EGON ALTDORF

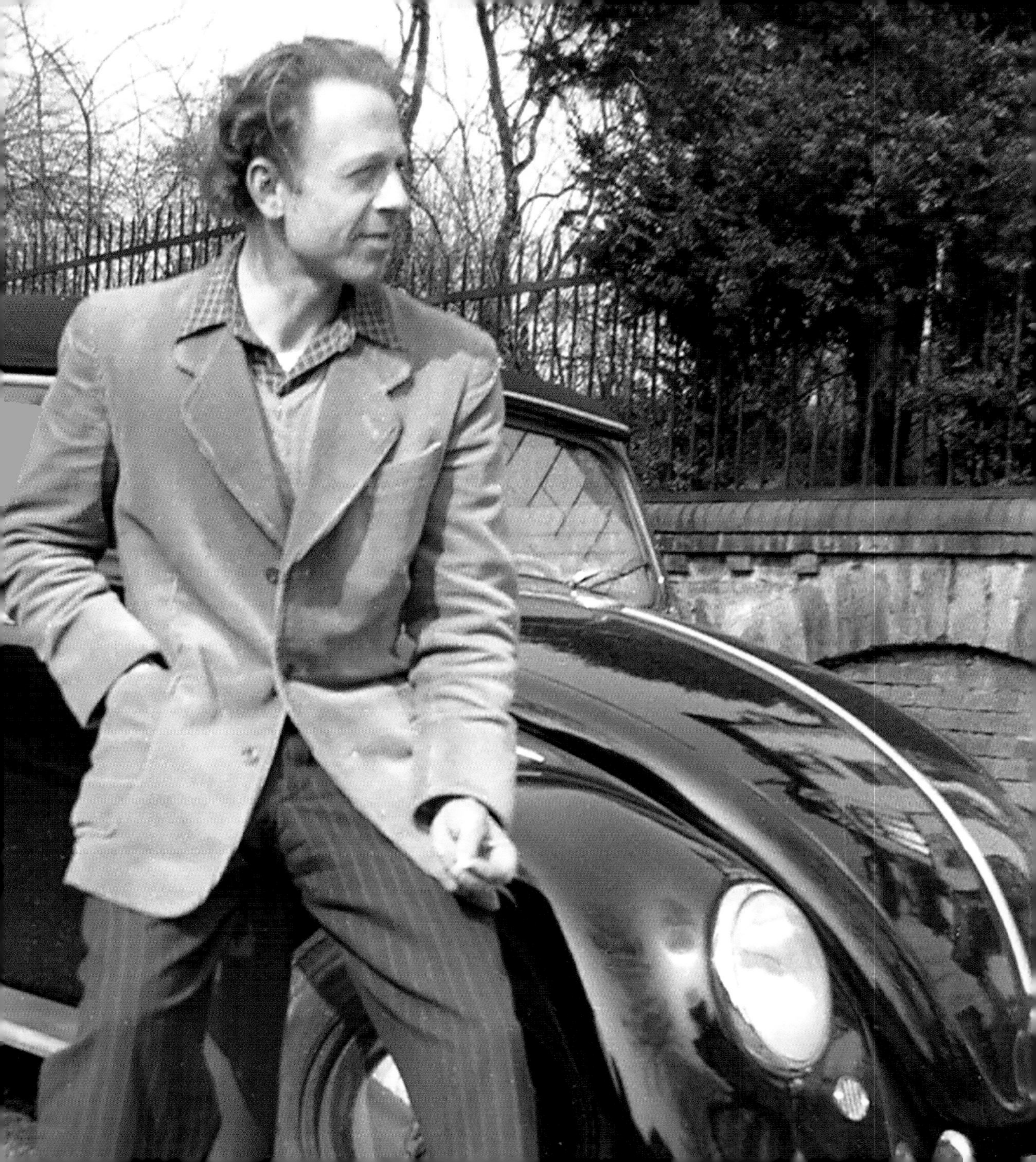

EGON ALTDORF

Poems + Images
Lyrik/Grafik/Skulptur

JUDITH LEGROVE

editor

MICHAEL TREVOR

translator

First published in 2023 by Sansom and Company,
a publishing imprint of Redcliffe Press Ltd.,
81g Pembroke Road, Bristol BS8 3EA
www.sansomandcompany.co.uk | info@sansomandcompany.co.uk

ISBN 978-1-915670-12-0
© The Estate of Egon Altdorf

Editor: Judith LeGrove
Translation: Michael Trevor
Design and typesetting by Simon Bishop
Printed and Bound in the UK by Short Run Press Ltd via Akcent Media

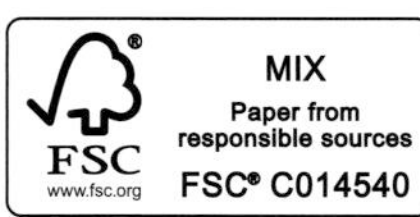

Sansom & Co is committed to being an environmentally friendly publisher.
This book is made from Forest Stewardship Council® certified paper.

Opposite: Egon Altdorf carving *Standing Man*, c. 1952

Title page: Egon Altdorf in Wiesbaden, c. 1957

Cover: Seated Man, 1952, bronze, 30 cm (high), location unknown

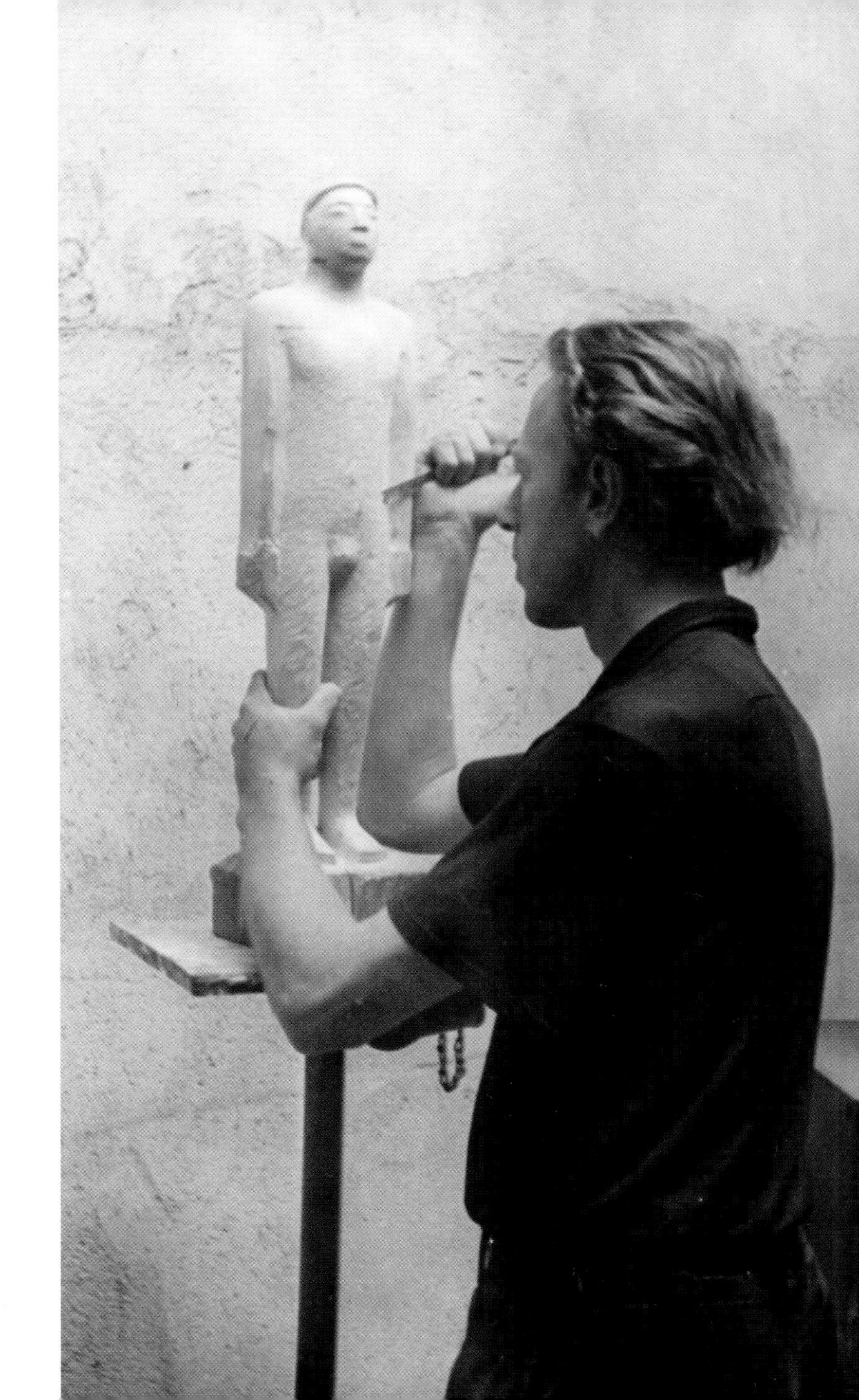

Contents

FOREWORD

Egon Altdorf (1922–2008) was a sculptor, printmaker, stained-glass designer and poet. Born in Treptow an der Rega, in East Pomerania, near the Baltic coast (now Trzebiatów in Poland), he grew up in Berlin, spending time in museums, libraries, art galleries, theatres and jazz clubs. He was conscripted into the Luftwaffe's communications unit in 1941, captured in north Africa in 1943 and spent two years in in the United States at Camp Mexia, Texas, as a prisoner of war. Having lost both parents, he chose to settle in Wiesbaden, working initially as a newspaper editor. From 1947 to 1951 he studied art in Wiesbaden and Mainz, learning to carve, to model in clay and plaster, and to make woodcuts from salvaged materials. His early works focused on the figure and on religious themes. In 1953, having won the Berlin Senate Prize for his entry to the Unknown Political Prisoner international sculpture competition, he travelled to London to see his maquette exhibited at the Tate. He visited Henry Moore's studio in Much Hadham and met several of Britain's most talented young sculptors, including Reg Butler, Lynn Chadwick, Eduardo Paolozzi and Geoffrey Clarke, the consequence of which was to direct his work towards abstraction.

Altdorf's outlook was open-spirited and humanitarian: shaped if not defined by his experience of war. Catholic by upbringing, he developed a profound connection with the Jewish community in Wiesbaden. He was commissioned in 1953 to create a memorial to the synagogue destroyed on *Kristallnacht* 1938, and when a new synagogue was planned he was invited to design its stained glass and sculptural fittings. This new synagogue in Wiesbaden, inaugurated in 1966, is now considered to be one of the finest examples of post-war synagogue architecture in Germany.

Reluctant to compromise, and preferring not to collaborate with galleries or dealers, Altdorf supported himself through teaching and commissions. Consequently, his work has until recently remained relatively unknown. A centenary exhibition in 2022 at Wiesbaden's Kunstarche (art archive), a book published in German (*Egon Altdorf 1922–2008: Die Kunst der inneren Erneuerung*, Reichert Verlag, 2022) and English (*Into the Light: The Art of Egon Altdorf*, Sansom, 2023), and further exhibitions in 2023 at the Henry Moore Institute, Leeds, and the University of Glasgow Memorial Chapel, have begun to alter this, making clear the strength and continuing resonance of his *oeuvre*.

Altdorf wrote poetry from the early 1940s until his death, leaving an extensive archive of unpublished manuscripts. Three volumes of poetry were published during his lifetime: *Circle of 7 Gates* (*Kreis der 7 Tore*, 1995), *Dream of Life* (*Traum vom Leben*, 2000) and *Way and Star* (*Weg und Stern*, 2001), each featuring an introduction, the first of which is reproduced here. This new anthology, *Poems + Images*, includes published and previously unpublished texts. Altdorf's earliest surviving poems, written in captivity, reflect upon war experience and art seen in Berlin; later poems occasionally address his own work. The images reproduced in this volume should be regarded not as illustrations to specific texts – although this is sometimes the case – but as a selection chosen to illuminate the constancy, invention and power of Altdorf's vision.

Altdorf spoke English and French fluently and described himself as 'European'. This first parallel edition of his poetry aims to introduce his written work to a wider audience.

Judith LeGrove

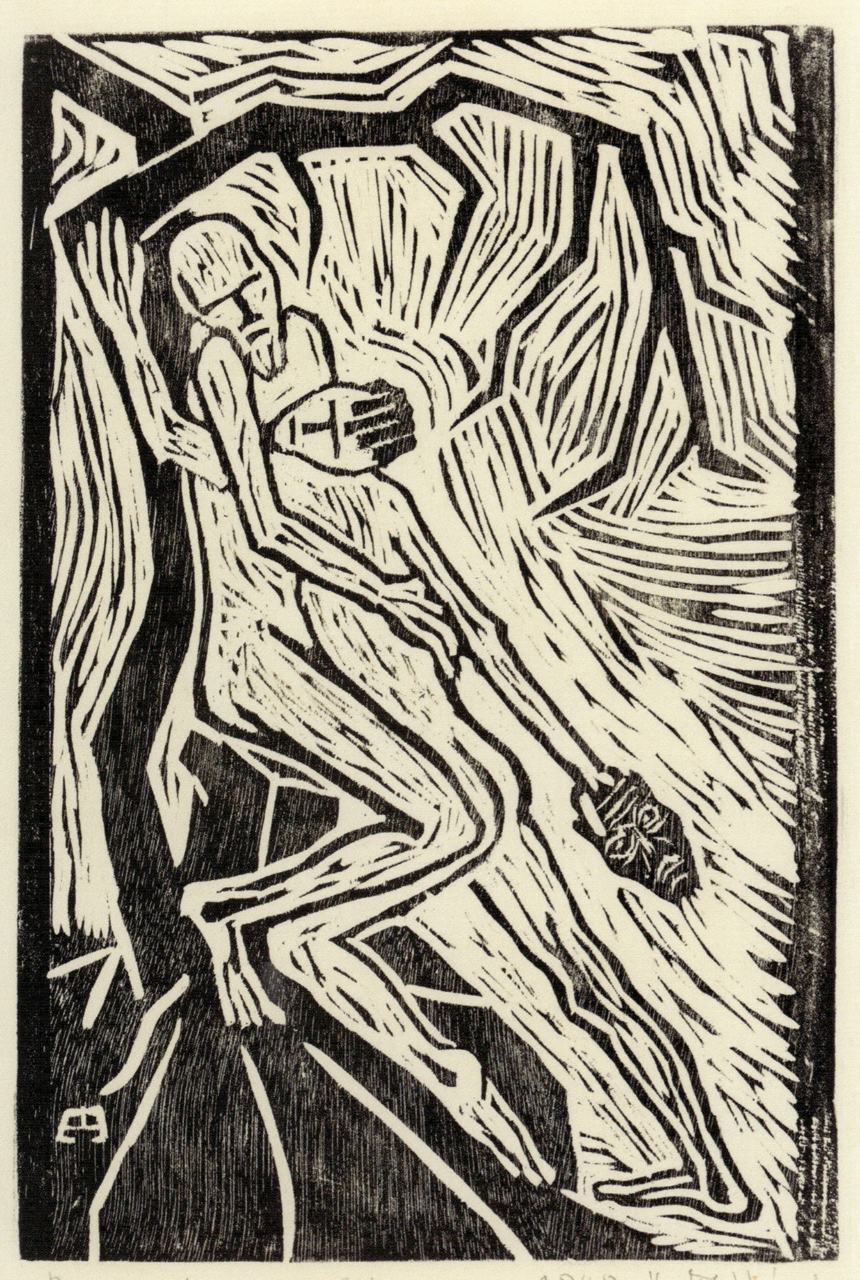

«Der verlorene Sohn»   1948 [signature]

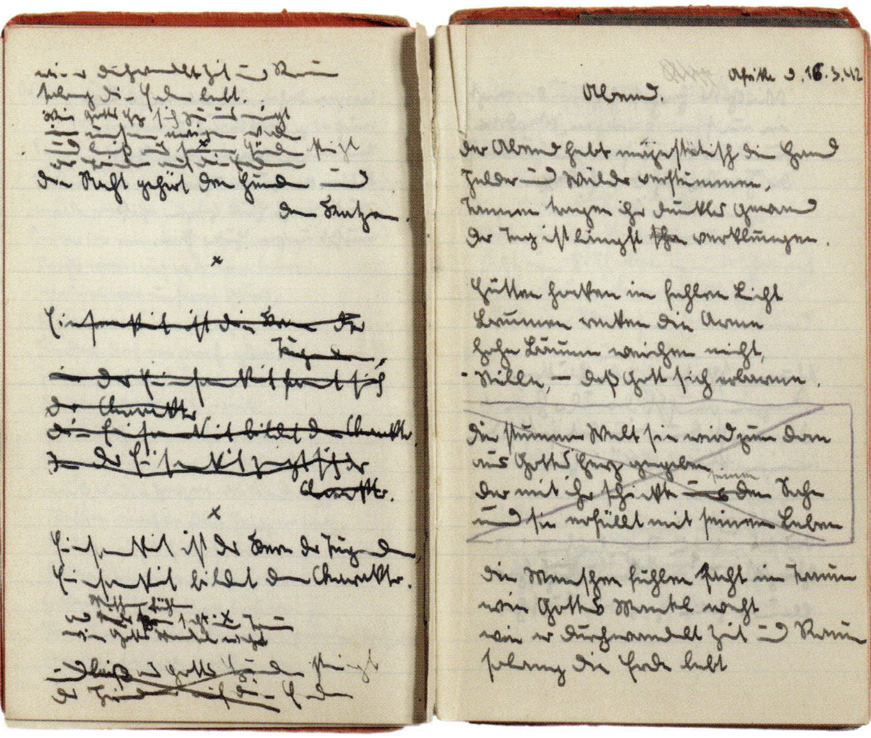

Egon Altdorf's poetry notebook,
1941–46

Opposite: **Der Verlorene Sohn**
The Prodigal Son
1948, woodcut, 31.5 x 21 cm

POEMS 1942-1945

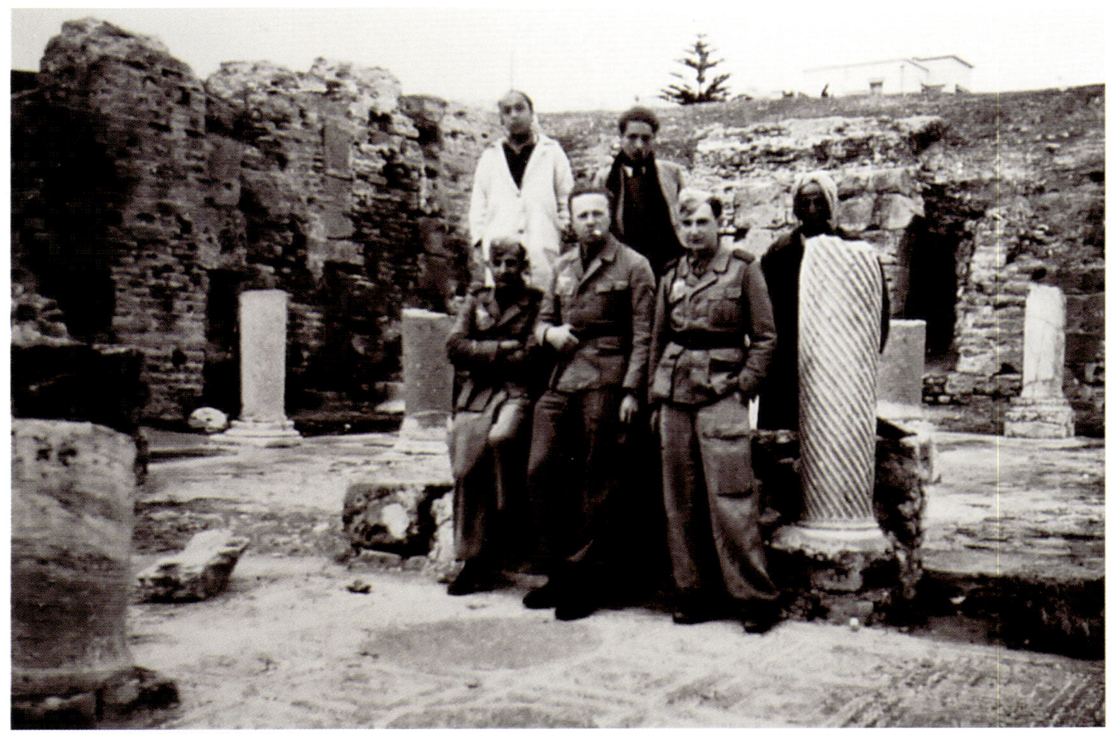

Egon Altdorf during military service in north Africa, c. 1942

Ich lag zwischen Felsen und träumte,
die Augen über mir gehörten
            einer grünen Echse,
die sich mit zitternden Flanken sonnte.

Sciacca, 17 November 1942

I lay between rocks, in a dream,
above me a pair of eyes that belonged
            to a green lizard,
his flanks trembling, sunning himself.*

Sciacca, 17 November 1942

Einsamkeit wollt' ich
und fand eine Ameise
die emsig ihre Eier trug.

Monte Lauro, 25 November 1942

I wanted solitude
and found an ant
busily carrying her eggs.

Monte Lauro, 25 November 1942

Erhabene, einsame Kathedrale.
Der Wind seufzt
            um die zerbrochenen Pfeiler
und um den Altar lärmen freche Spatzen.

Naro, 28 November 1942

Sublime, lonely cathedral.
The wind sighs
            around broken pillars
and cheeky sparrows squabble round the altar.

Naro, 28 November 1942

Sieh, nur eine Schneeflocke!
Doch tausend kleine Sterne
halte ich in meiner Hand.

Dezember 1942

Look, just a snowflake!
But a thousand little stars
held in my hand.

December 1942

*In the fairytale within Novalis's novel *Die Lehrlinge zu Saïs*, a lizard appears and sings a short, happy song: 'das Eidexchen geschlüpft kam, sich auf einem warmen Stein setzte, mit dem Schwanzchen wedelte und sang' ('the lizard tipped up, settled himself on a warm stone, wagged his tail and sang').

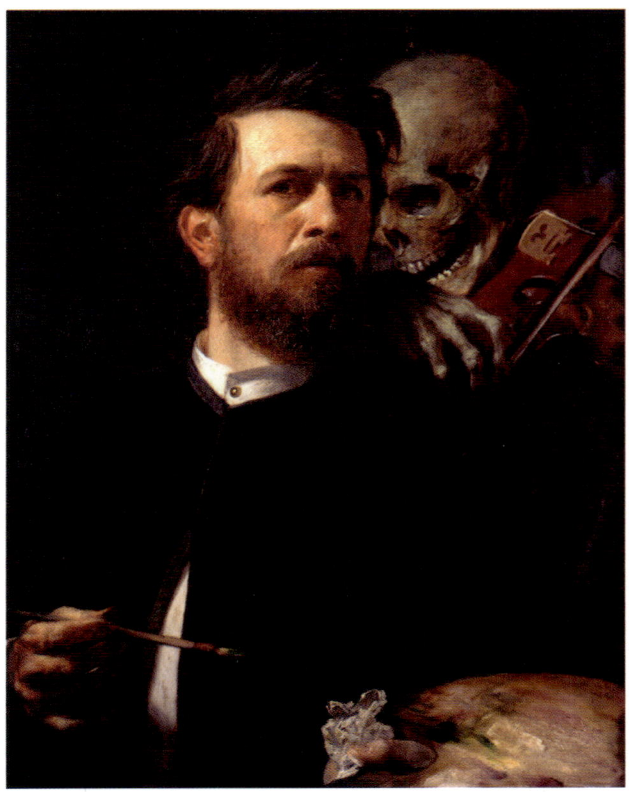

Arnold Böcklin, Selbstbildnis mit fiedelndem Tod
Arnold Böcklin, Self-Portrait with Death Playing the Fiddle
1872, oil on canvas, 75 x 61 cm, Nationalgalerie, Berlin

MANN UND TOD
Zu Arnold Böcklin's
„Selbstbildnis mit Tod"

Lausche nur Mann,
der Tod führt an
hurtig und geigt
Vergessenheit.

Leben und Zeit
wird Dir gegeigt,
Dein Atem verklingt
eh die Saite noch springt.

Bist nun berührt,
emsig gerührt,
hast zu vollenden
mit ruhlosen Händen.

Trotze ihm ab
die Zeit bis zum Grab,
Dein Werk wird sein
noch über dem Stein.

8 März 1944

MAN AND DEATH
On Arnold Böcklin's
'Self-Portrait with Death'

Man, learn from me,
Death leads you on
his quickstep to
oblivion.

Your span on earth
will soon be spent,
his leaping strings
outlast your breath.

Be stirred now, fired
to persevere,
untiring till
your task be done.

Wrest from his grip
what time is left,
your work shall live
and cheat the grave.

8 March 1944

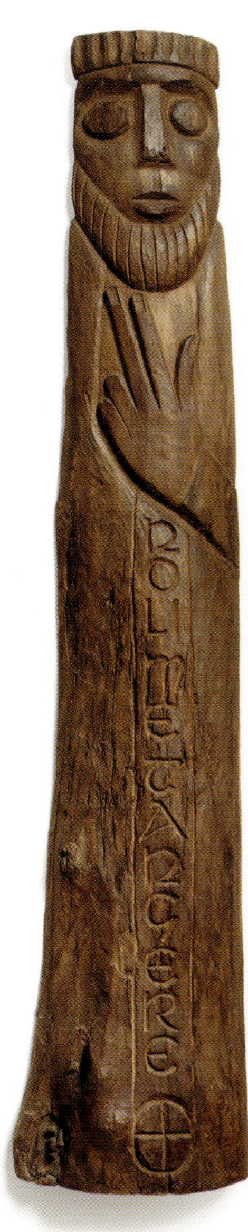

Noli me tangere
1947, wood, 140 x 25 cm

Ich will
wie ein Baum
fest
in der Erde ruh'n,

doch meine Zweige
sind
im Wind,

bis das Licht
mich
zerbricht.

April / Mai 1944

I would rest
like a tree,
fast
in the earth

but my branches
shake
in the wind

till the light
breaks me.

April / May 1944

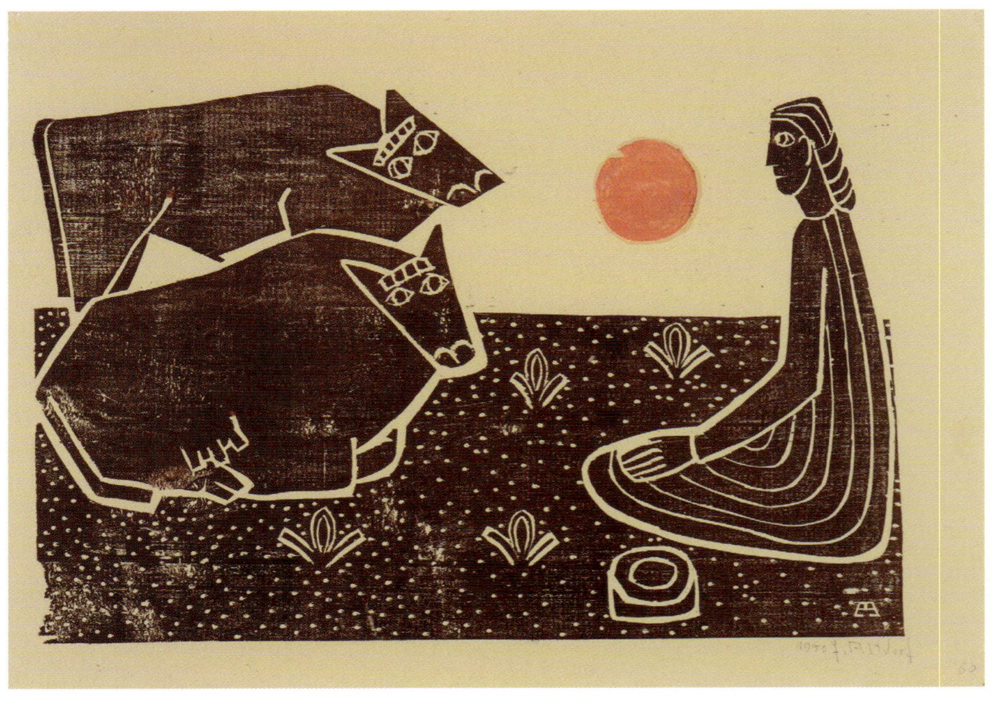

Frau mit Rindern und roter Sonne
Woman with Cattle and Red Sun
1950, woodcut, 40 x 62 cm

ABEND

Nun steht
die Stille
wie eine Wand
im Land.

Nur durch die Fülle
des Schweigens weht
ein letztes Licht
wie Händereichen,

das von den weichen,
müden Lauten
kleiner Tiere
zag begleitet,

sich groß zum letzten Brande weitet
und
verlischt.

9 Mai 1944

EVENING

Now stands
the stillness
cliff-like
on the land.

While through the fullness
of the silence drifts
a last light
like hands outstretched,

and timidly
accompanied
by the hushed, sleepy sounds
of small animals,

widens out to its last great flame
and
is quenched.

9 May 1944

Die Nacht
wird wie ein Dom
im Schweigen,

doch fühlst du
lebend
rings
die Stille atmen,

du möchtest
sehnsuchtsvoll
die Arme breiten

und in den weiten,
stillen Dingen,

ein Stück
von ihnen
sein.

30 Mai 1944

The night
in its silence
becomes like a cathedral,

and yet you feel,
around you,
living,
the stillness breathe,

and longingly
you might
stretch out your arms

and among
the vast, still things,

be
part
of them.

30 May 1944

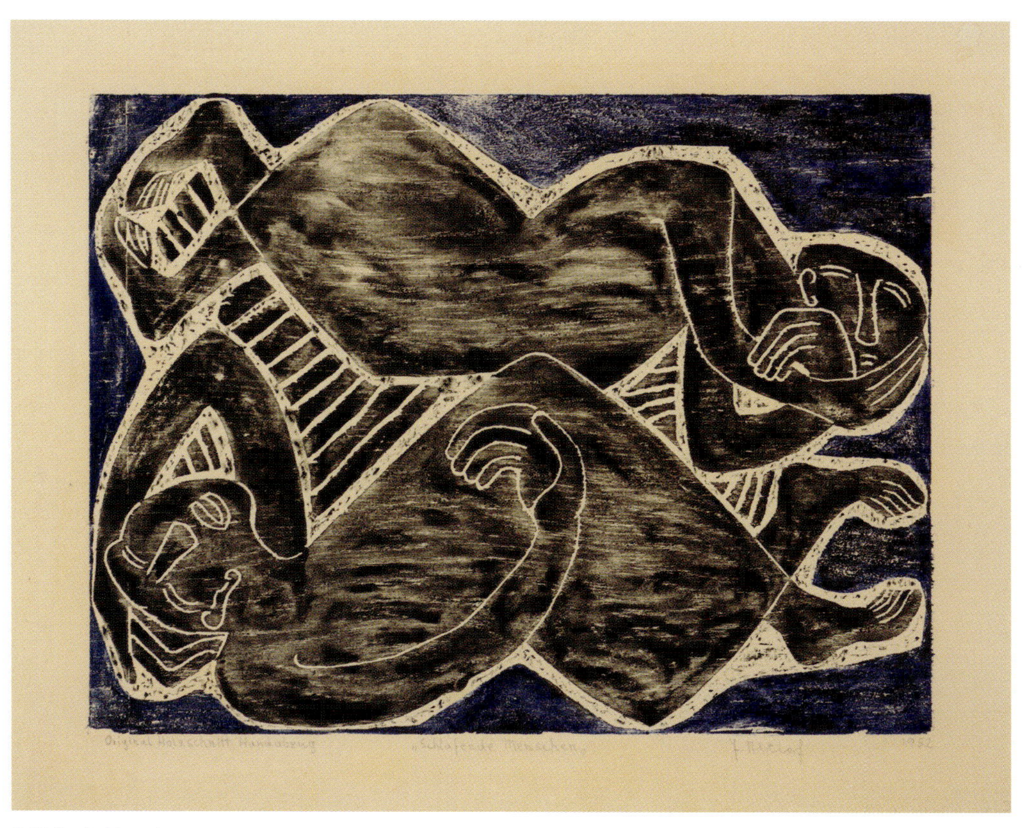

Schlafende Menschen
Sleeping Figures
1952, woodcut, 41.5 x 54.5 cm

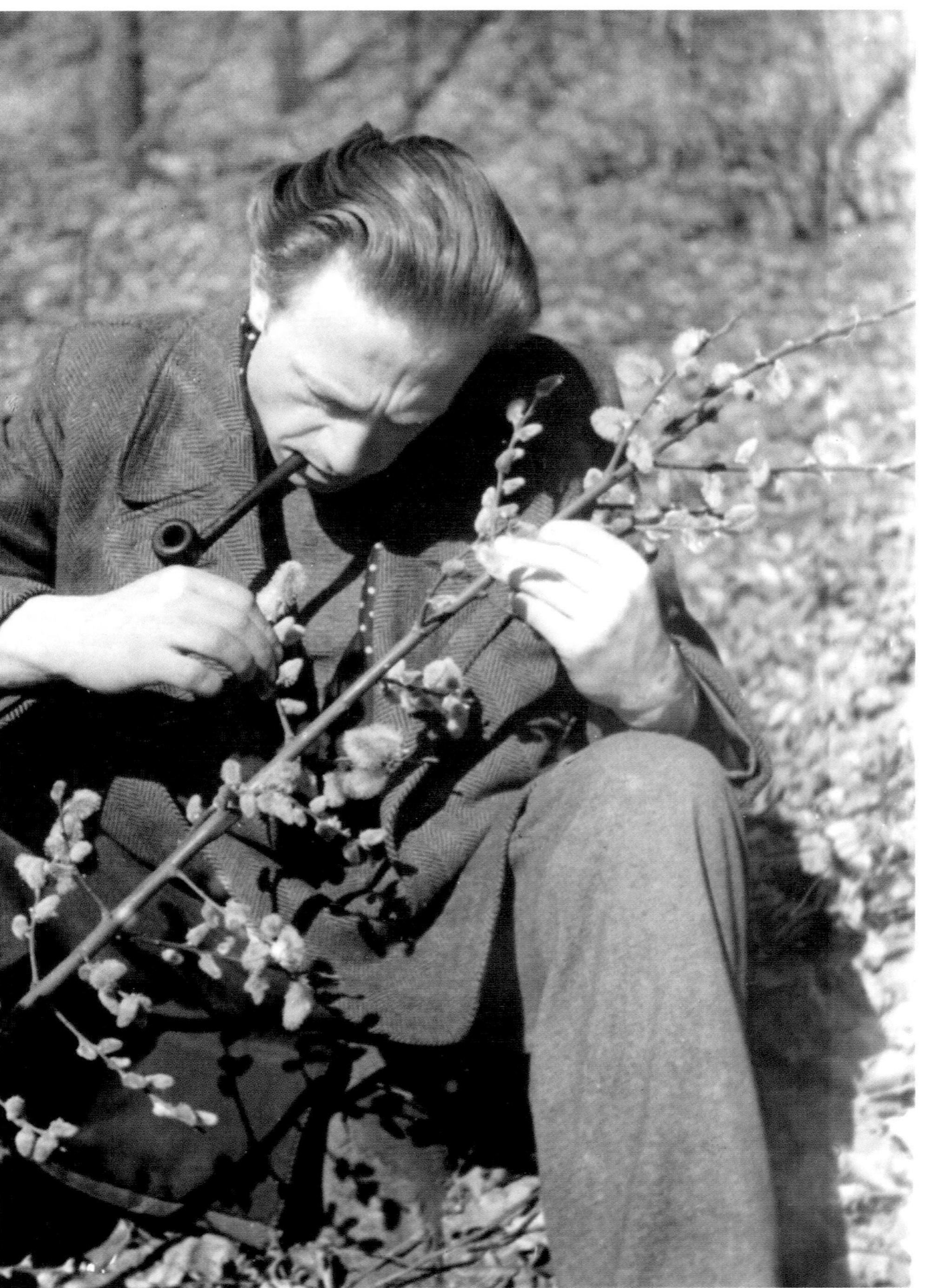

Vor meinem Fenster
steht ein junger Baum
grad so,
dass deine kleinen Zweige
ein wenig
über das Gesimse schaun.
Wenn ich erwache
ist sein erster Gruss an mich,
er winkt mich freundlich
in den kühlen Morgenschatten.
Und wenn ich abends
mich zur Ruh begebe,
grüsst er mich noch,
gut Nacht mein Freund,
und zittert zierlich
mit den jungen Blättern.

9 Juni 1944, Mexia Hospital (Malaria)

Outside my window
stands a young tree,
so that
your little branches
can just
be seen above the cornice.
When I wake up
his first greeting
is a friendly wave
in the cool morning shadows.
And in the evening
when it's time to rest,
he greets me again,
Goodnight my friend,
and delicately flutters
his young leaves.

9 June 1944, Mexia Hospital (Malaria)

Egon Altdorf, c. 1957

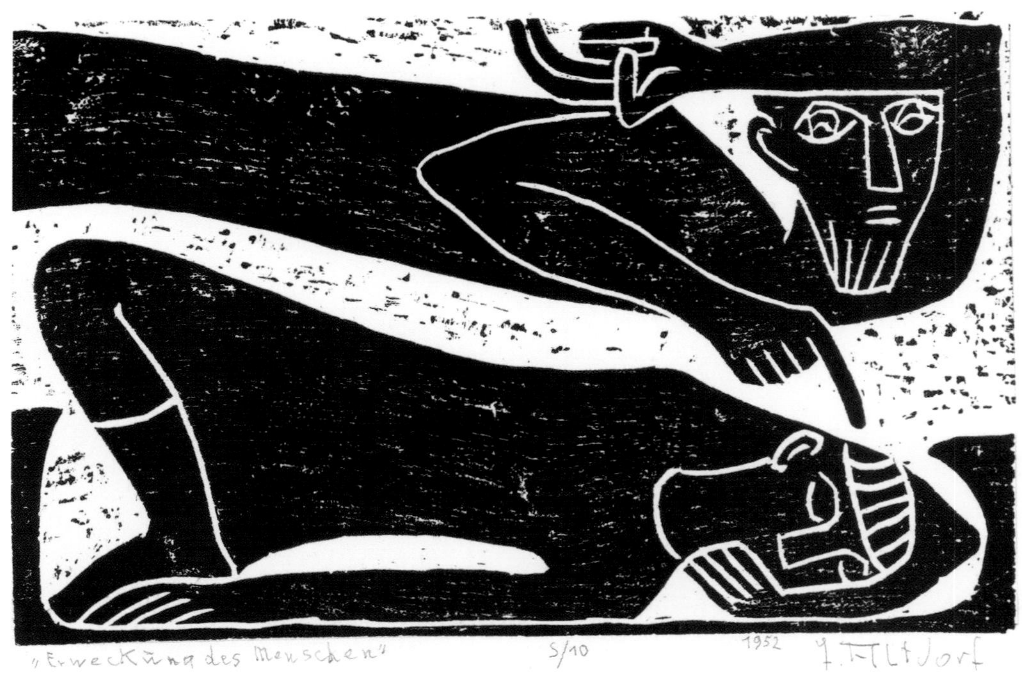

Erweckung des Menschen
Awakening of Man
1952, woodcut, 15.5 x 31 cm

ZU RILKES „DUINESER ELEGIEN"

Wer Rilke liest
muss anders seine Hände halten,
als walten
neuen Weltenkräfte rings im Äther.
Wie neugeboren
wirfst du alte Kleider fort,
ein neues Wort,
das niemand je so ganz gefunden,
das doch um dich in allen Dingen ruht,
liegt nun bereit zu deinen Füssen.

Nur sieh dich vor,
dass nicht die Spitze deines Fusses es berührt,
du musst dich neigen, wie es ihm gebührt
und ganz und ganz
dein Herz zu deinen Füssen legen.

2 Dezember 1944

ON RILKE'S 'DUINO ELEGIES'

To read Rilke,
is to hold your hands otherwise,
as new cosmic powers
rule in the ether around you.
As when reborn,
you throw away old clothes,
a new word,
that no one has ever so completely found,
yet quietly surrounds you in all things,
now sits expectantly at your feet.

Only take care
that the tip of your foot not touch it,
you must bow down, as is fitting,
and wholly, wholly
lay your heart at your feet.

2 December 1944

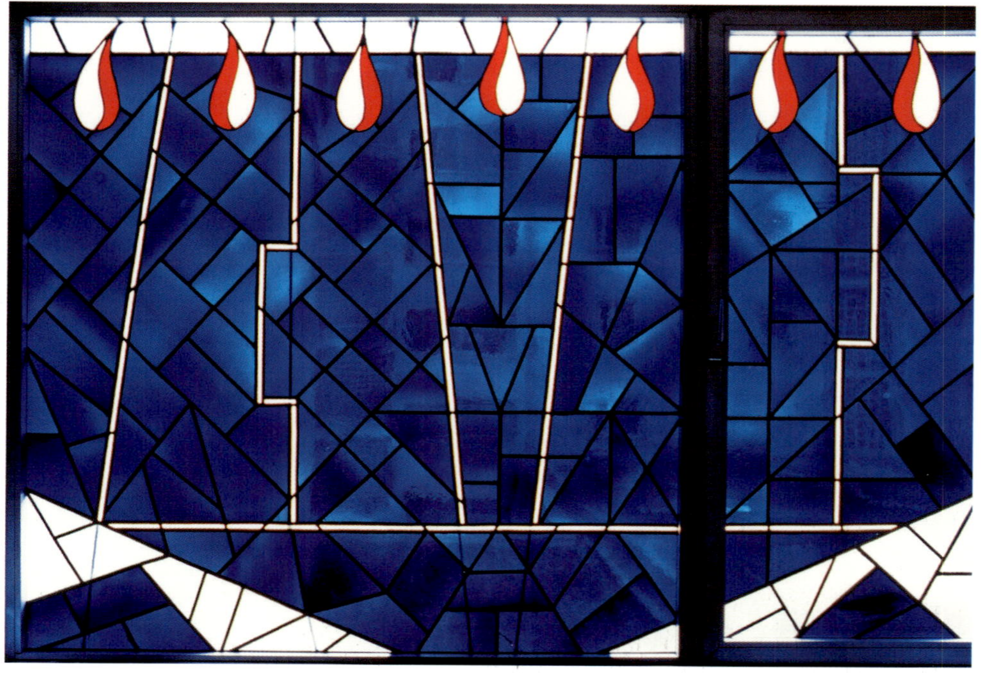

Window in the stairwell of the new synagogue, Wiesbaden, 1966

Geschrieben in der Weihnachtsnacht
am Stacheldraht (im Lichte einer Bogenlampe)

Ohn' Baum und Licht
ist nicht
ein Mensch auf dieser Erden.

Der Baum bist du,
das Licht dazu
kann nur aus deinem Herzen werden.

24 Dezember 1944, 2300 Uhr

Written on Christmas Eve by the barbed wire
(in the light of an arc lamp)

But for this tree
and light,
there'd be no soul on earth.

You are that tree,
its light
comes only from your heart.

24 December 1944, 11 p.m.

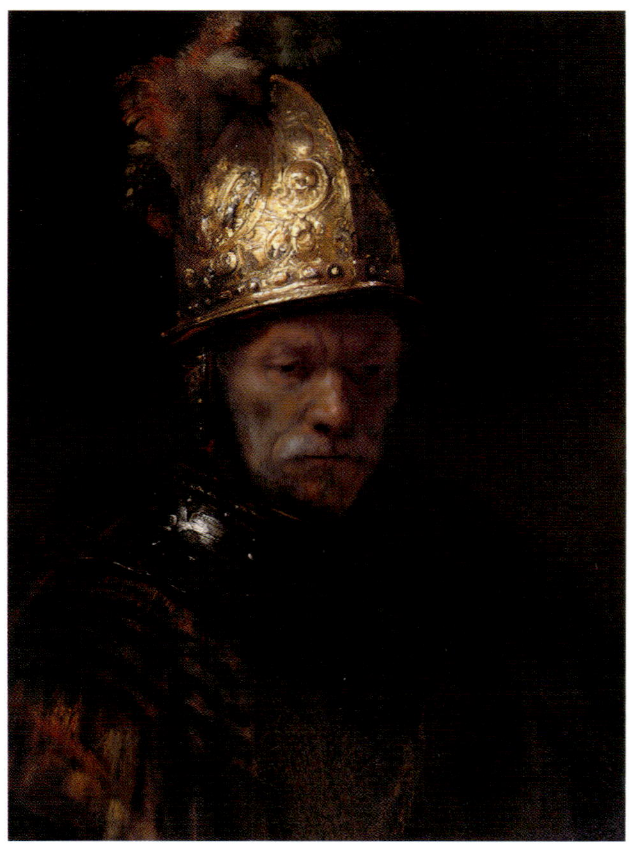

Rembrandt (ehemalige Zuschreibung), Der Mann mit dem Goldhelm
Rembrandt (former attribution), The Man with the Golden Helmet
1650/60, oil on canvas, 67.5 x 50.7 cm, Gemäldegalerie, Berlin

ZU REMBRANDTS GEMÄLDE
„DER MANN MIT DEM GOLDENEN HELM"

Wie frostig blickts Du aus dem Dunkel,
das Dich wohl ungern zu vermissen scheint,
die Hälfte Deines Antlitz nur
gibst Du dem hellen Licht,
unwillig, trotzig, kühl erwägend,
als hätte Dunkel Dich so grau versteint.

Das Hellste an Dir aber ist:
Dein goldener Helm,
ein kalter Schimmer Deiner Rüstung,
das kleine Blinken einer Schnalle,
die Dir getreu Dein Sturmband hält.

Kein Strahlen bricht aus Deinen Augen,
nichts spricht aus Dir von Glanz und Pracht,
auf allen Deinen starken Zügen
liegt stumme Härte, tiefe Nacht.

Wenn Du mir lebend aus dem Bilde trätest,
bät ich um Deine harten Hände,
ich würde nichts mir sonst erwählen,
als nur:
Dein Weggenosse sein zu dürfen
durch Dunkelheit zur hellen Wende.

25 Januar 1945

ON REMBRANDT'S PAINTING
'THE MAN WITH THE GOLDEN HELMET' *

How frostily you look at us out of the darkness
from which you seem reluctant to emerge,
offering just half your countenance
to the full light:
guarded, coolly appraising, thrawn,
as if the darkness had turned you to this grey stone.

But here is where the light is brightest on you:
your golden helmet,
your armour's cold shimmer,
a glint on the buckle
that secures your chinstrap.

No radiance breaks from your eyes,
nothing in you speaks of lustre or splendour,
the strong lines of your face show only
hardness, reticence, deep night.

If you stepped living out of the picture towards me,
I would plead for your hard hands,
but would ask nothing else,
only
to be your companion on the road through the darkness
to the bright turning point.

25 January 1945

* Altdorf would have known this painting, which is now ascribed
to a follower of Rembrandt, from his childhood in Berlin.

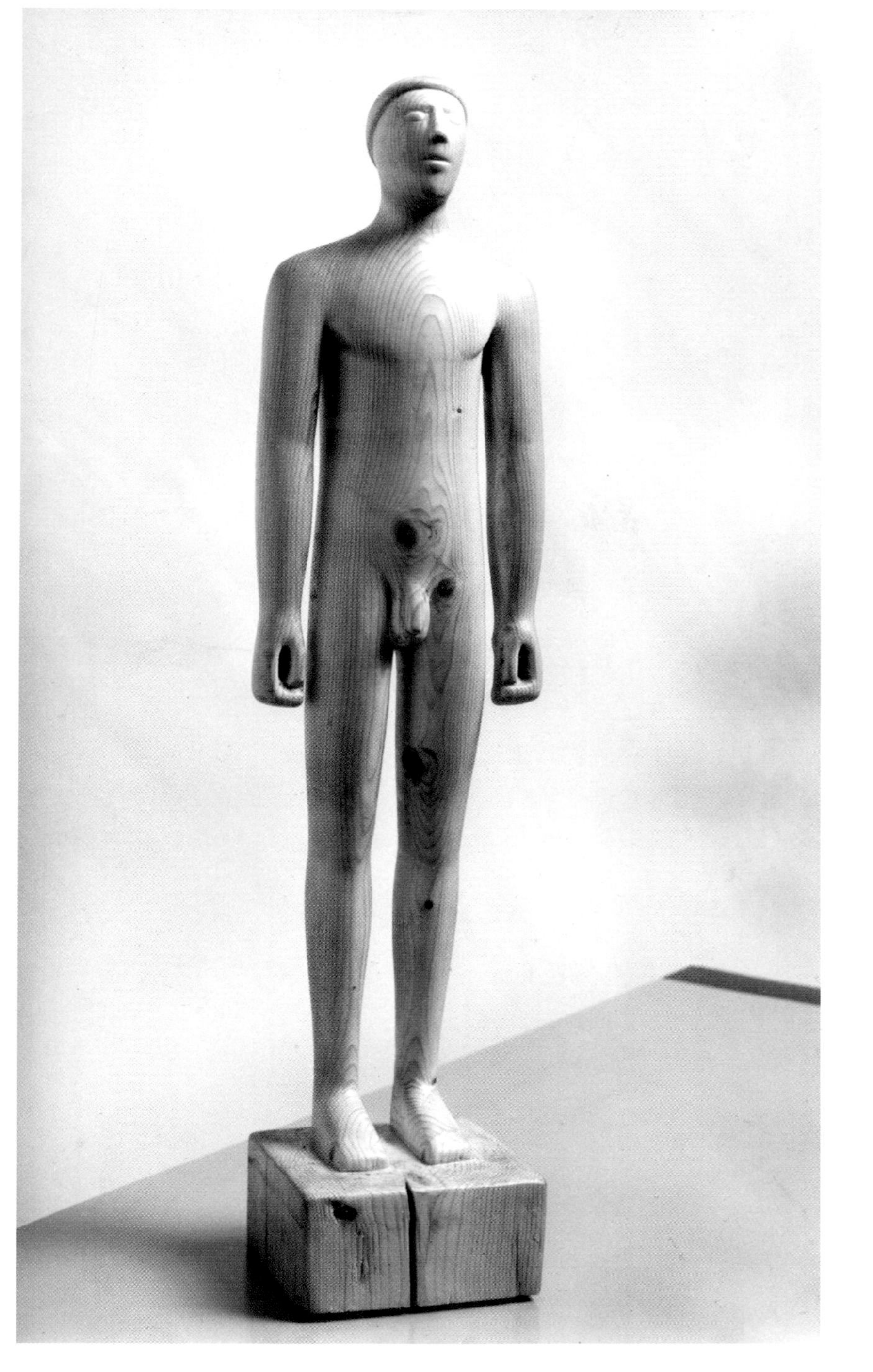

OSTSEE

An meinem Meere will ich wieder stehen
und es muss Nacht sein,
Dunkel weit,
nur deine Stimme will ich hören,
die wie Choräle Domesmauern zittern macht.

     Ich will gebannt
vor deiner dunklen Urmacht weilen,
wie im Gebet vor deiner Allmacht stehen,
bis ich durch deine Lebenskraft gebenedeit
ganz zu den stillen Wäldern hingenesen,
vor jeder fremden Sehnsucht bin befreit,
und will mit kindlich, gläubigem Wesen
still, dankbar durch die Felder gehen.

2 Oktober 1945

BALTIC

I want to stand again beside my sea
and it must be night, distant and dark,
I want
only to hear your voice, which like chorales
can shake cathedral walls.

     I'd stand enthralled
by your dark universal power, until
blessed by your living force,
healed and restored
to the silent woods and freed
from every strange longing,
I'd walk, faithful and childlike,
in gratitude and stillness, through the fields.

2 October 1945

Stehender Mann
Standing Man
1952, wood, 55 x 12.5 x 13 cm, Museum Wiesbaden

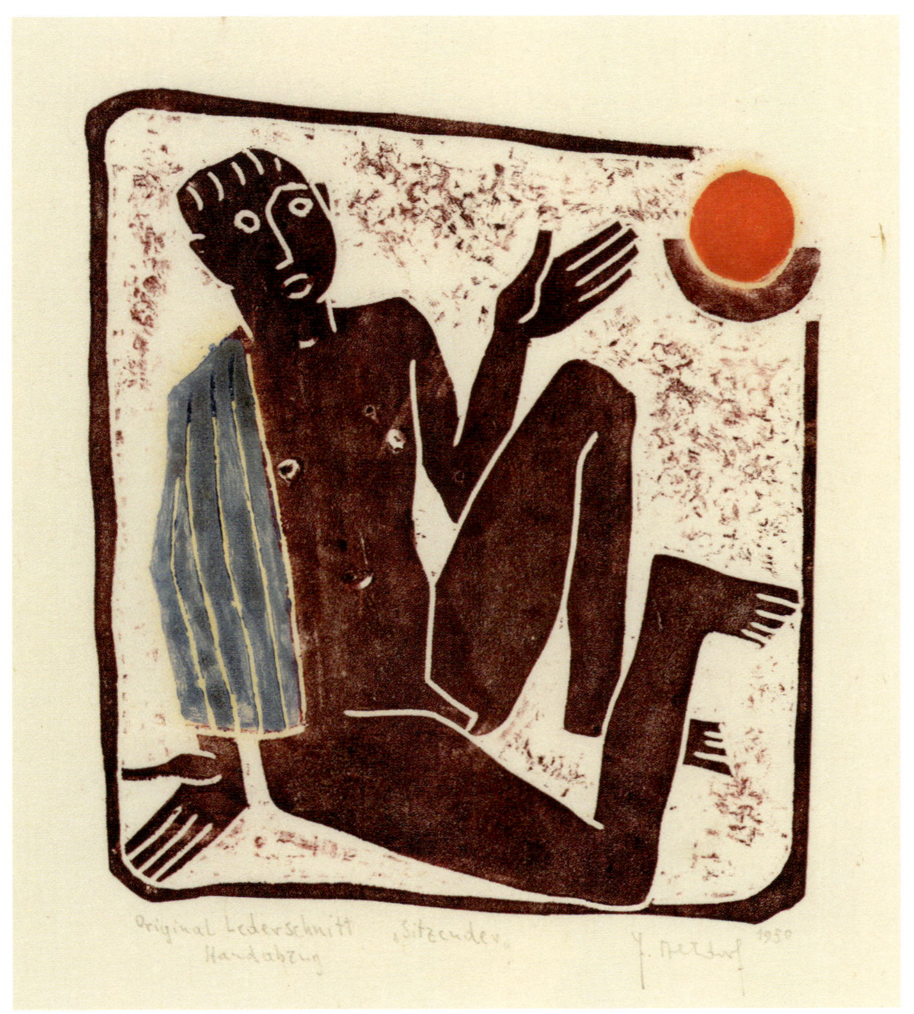

Sitzender
Seated Man
1950, leathercut, 20 x 19 cm

Opposite: **Schlafende**
Sleeping Woman
1951, leathercut, 19 x 18.5 cm

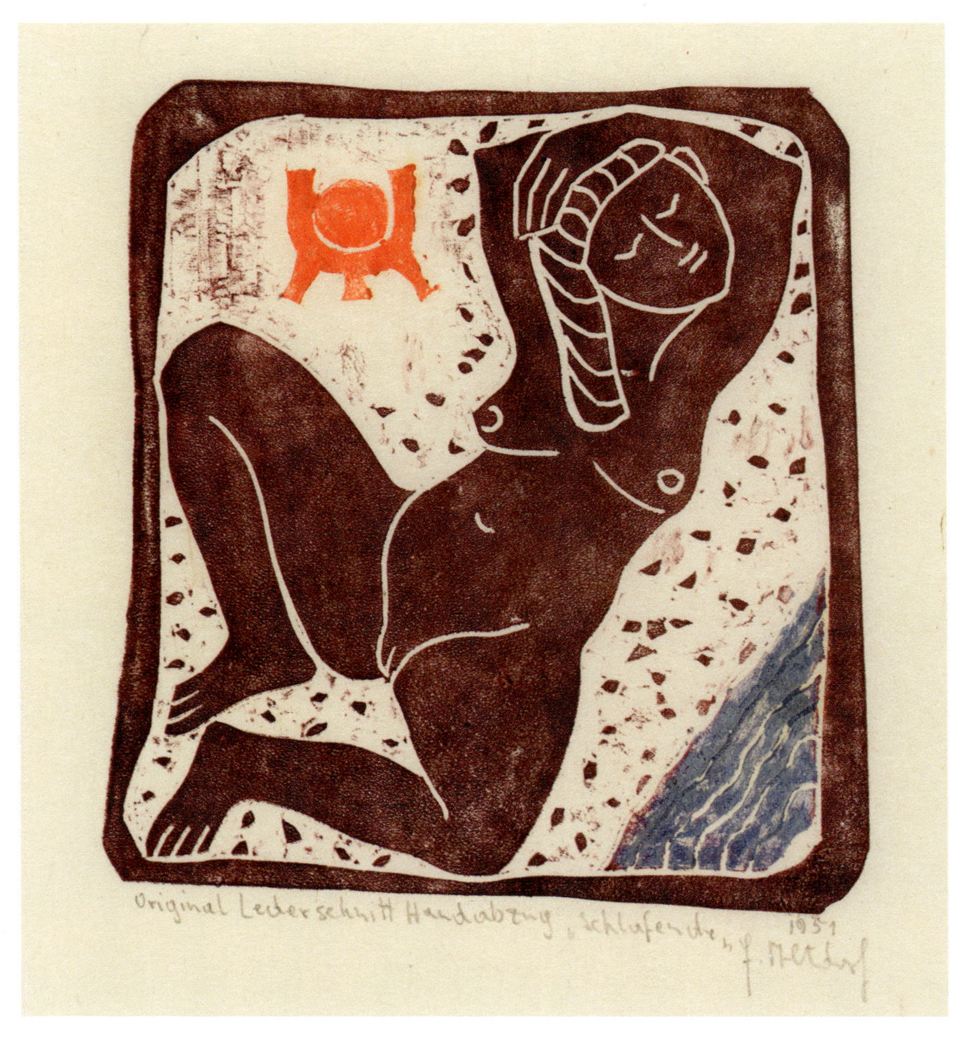

ORIGINS

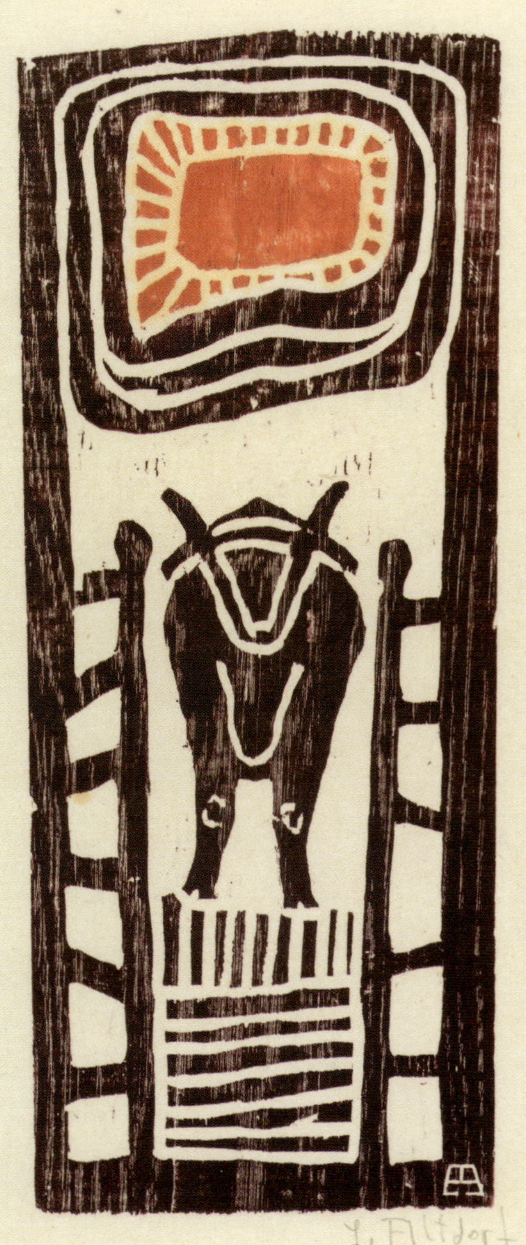

Ochse
Ox
1949, woodcut, 35 x 14.5 cm

MEIN HERKOMMEN

Als ich noch goldener Hirte war,
am weichen silbernen Fluß
im Osten

und milde Kühle
atmend fand,
zum heißen Mittag,
in dornigen Gebüschen,

dort am hellen Wasser,
in heißer, schweigender,
weiter Landschaft,

die gierig trinkenden Rinder,
ihre gehörnten Köpfe neigend,
in den Wolkenhimmelfluß.

Meine Hirtentasche
mit dem bäuerlichen Brot.

Dort hielt ich
in meiner Knabenhand
die goldene Sonnenscheibe
der Welt.

Barfüßig zog ich
im heißen Staube des Weges,
behutsam,
hinter der langsam,
heimschwankenden Herde.

MY ORIGIN

When I was still a golden herdsman
by the soft silver river
in the East

and breathing mild coolness
found
towards the hot noon,
in thorny bushes,

there by the bright water
in that silent, hot,
wide landscape,

the thirsty drinking cattle,
bowing their horned heads,
in the cloudy sky river.

My herdsman's bag
with the rough farm bread.

There I held
in my small hand
the golden sun-disc
of the world.

Barefoot I walked
in the hot dust of the road,
watchful,
behind the slow, swaying
homebound herd.

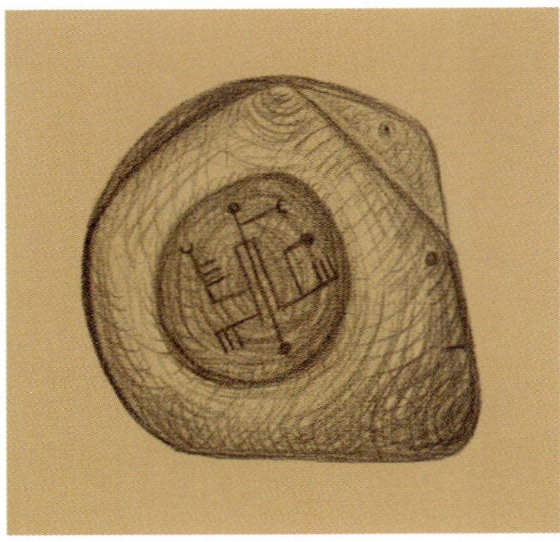

Holzmotiv
Wood motif
c. 1953, charcoal on paper, 25 x 26 cm

Was hat in diese Zweifel mich verbannt,
noch fühle ich den goldenen Staub
der schwingenden Unendlichkeit,
wie einen letzten Gruß aus frühen Händen.

Der Wind war mein Bruder,
die Sonne mein Keim,
aus Erdengluten ward mein Blut,
den Himmel hieß ich liebend „Vater".

Nun ist der Stern in meiner Brust
ein Fleisch gewordenes Herz,
mein Hirn, ein vages kurzes Spiel.

Ich recke erdenschwere Glieder,
als riefe wer,
als rief der Andere,
der Ich einst wohl war.

What banished me to these doubts,
I still feel the golden dust
the resonant infinity,
like a last greeting from familiar hands.

The wind was my brother,
the sun my seed,
my blood came from the heat of the earth,
the sky I lovingly called 'Father'.

Now is the star in my breast
a heart made flesh,
my brain, a vague short game.

I stretch earth-heavy limbs,
as if someone were calling to me,
the call of that Other,
that I once was.

Weitgeöffnetes Tor der Nacht,
in meine wartende zeitlose Heimat.

Schatten der Schritte,
die Splitter der Sterne,
kristallene Spreu
stacheln den Brand
der sprühenden Sehnsucht.

Mit dem Geflecht mondalter Sinne
umspann ich die Welt,
ein gläsernes Spielzeug.

Brüderlich fühl' ich
Herzatem der Nächte
früher Kulturen
und dämmernde Zeiten,
Verheißung der Liebe.

So ziehe ich zeitlos,
befreit vom Staube,
getragen im Nachtwind
mein Spiegel der Seele.

Wandernde Weisheit
ferner Gezeiten
spüre ich trostvoll
im Mondrausch der Räume.

Gate of night, thrown open into
my waiting timeless homeland.

Shadows of footsteps,
splinters of stars,
crystalline chaff
spark the spitting
flame of longing.

With the weave of moon-aged senses
I span the world,
a glass plaything.

Brotherly I feel
heart's breath of nights,
of older cultures,
and times of dusk or half light,
a promise of love.

So I pass timeless,
freed from the dust,
borne on the night wind,
my mirror of the soul.

Consoled, I sense
a wandering wisdom
of distant tides
in the moon-ecstasy of spaces.

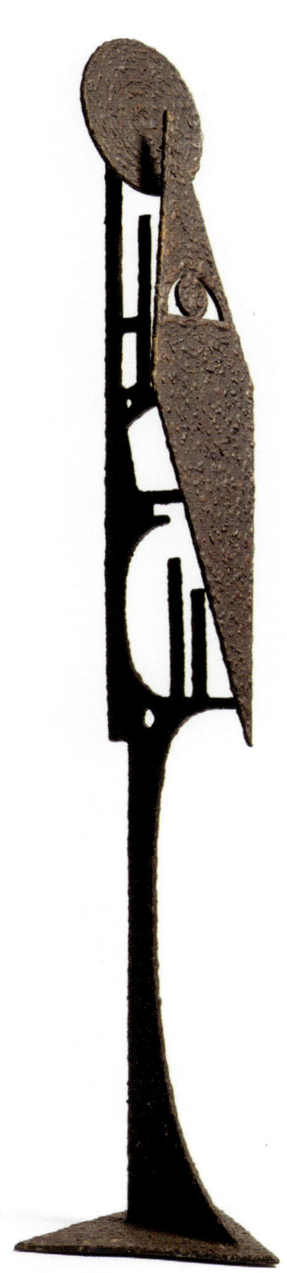

Kopfidol mit Scheibe
Head-Idol with Disc
1958, steel, 98 x 19 x 22 cm

TRAUM

In unserer alten Schmiede
sah ich als Knabe
das glühende Eisen,

auf dem festgefügten Amboß,
geformt unter dem Schlag des Hammers.

Dort stieg heiß in mir auf,
aus dem lodernden Feuer,
die Liebe zu formen,

eine Blüte zu schmieden
unter den Augen Gottes.

Ich träumte
von dem heiligen Schmied
vom Beginn der Erde.

Aus dem Klang
des geschmiedeten Eisen
wurde mein Traum,

von einer anderen Welt,
die aus dem heiligen Feuer kam.

DREAM

As a boy,
in our old smithy,
I saw the glowing iron,

formed by hammer blows
on the rock-solid anvil.

The leaping flames
kindled in me a burning
desire to shape, to form,

to forge a flower
under the eyes of God.

I dreamed
of the holy blacksmith
of the earth's beginning.

With the clang
of forged iron,
my dream became

that of another world,
that came from the holy fire.

<table>
<tr><td>

BLAUER TAG

Weit, in der blauen Weite
des Himmels,
schwingen die sanften
blauen Hügel der Wälder.

Die blaue Himmelsscheibe,
unendlich kreist
über den mächtigen,
blauen, schimmernden Wassern.

Das liebliche blaue Gewand,
der blaue schützende Sternenmantel
der lächelnden Himmelskönigin,
ist das Firmament,

Oh, süße Maria,

ihre geöffneten Hände
geben den Segen
und die Stille
des blauen Tages.

</td><td>

BLUE DAY

Deep, in the blue depths
of the sky,
sway the gentle
blue wooded hills.

The blue disc of the sky
circles, unending,
over the mighty,
blue, shimmering waters.

The lovely blue robe,
the blue sheltering starry cloak
of Heaven's smiling queen,
is the firmament,

O, sweet Mary,

your open hands
bestow the blessing
and the stillness
of the blue day.

</td></tr>
</table>

Altdorf's wife, Diana, with their son, Dorian,
in Wiesbaden, c. 1957

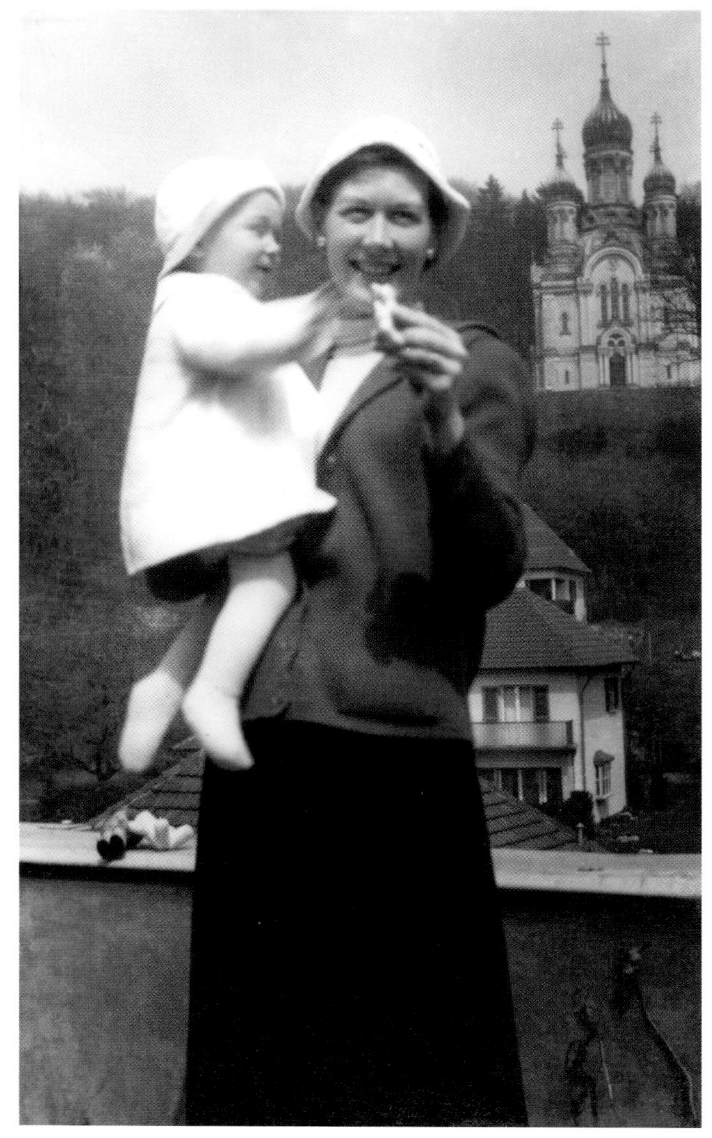

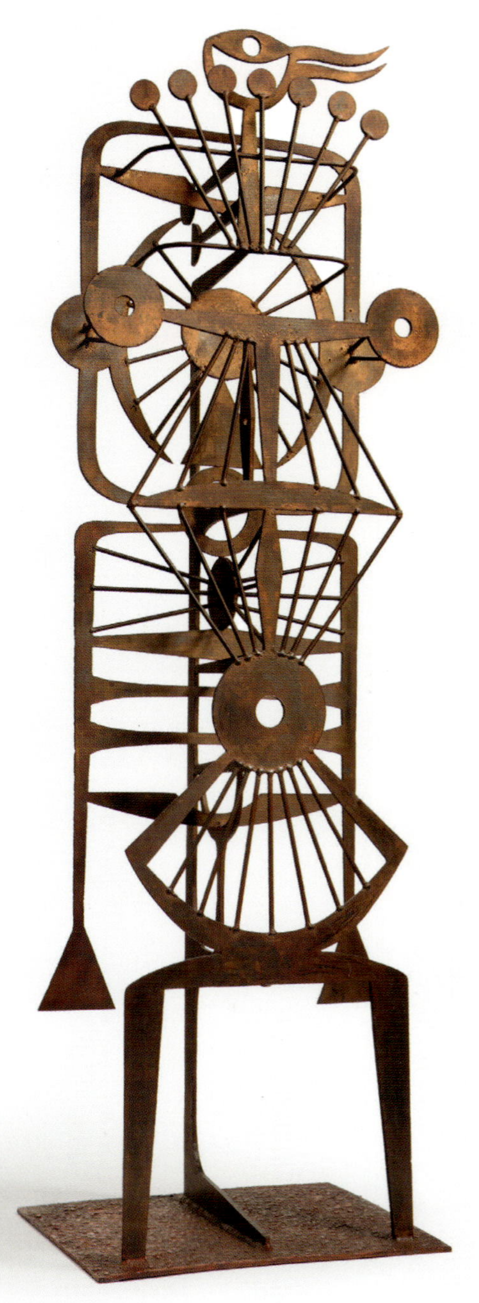

Wächter der Gestirne
Guardian of the Stars
1957, steel, painted red and gold,
120 x 37.5 x 30 cm

FUGE

Es fallen Töne
aus dem Raum,
wie rotes Erz.

Gebannt steht Einer,
wie im Traum.

Es sang nur
Gottes Klopfen
sich tiefer
in sein Herz.

FUGUE

Notes fall
from the air,
like red ore.

Spellbound, a man stands
as in a dream.

Only the song,
the knocking sound of God,
sang itself deeper
into his heart.

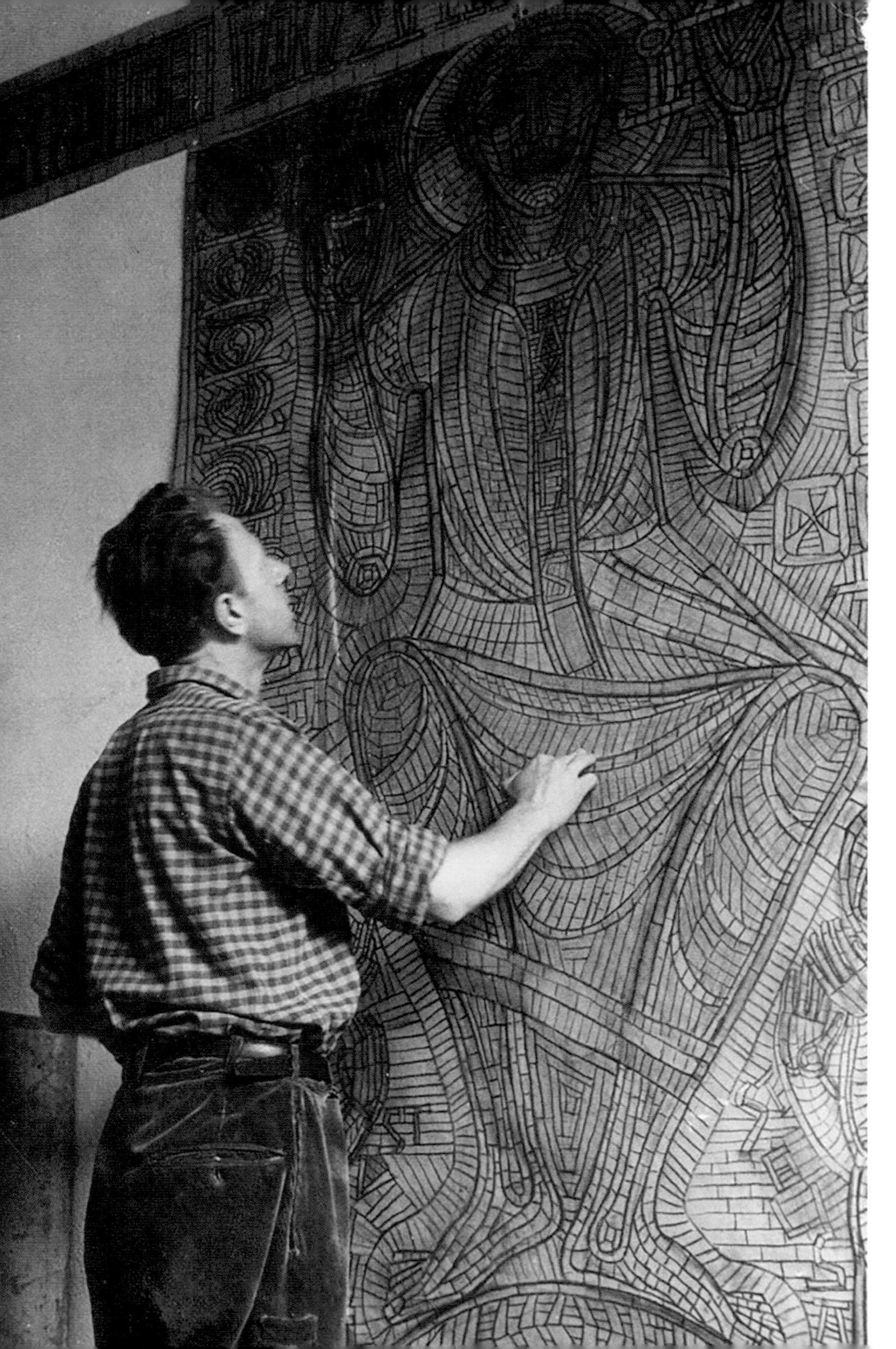

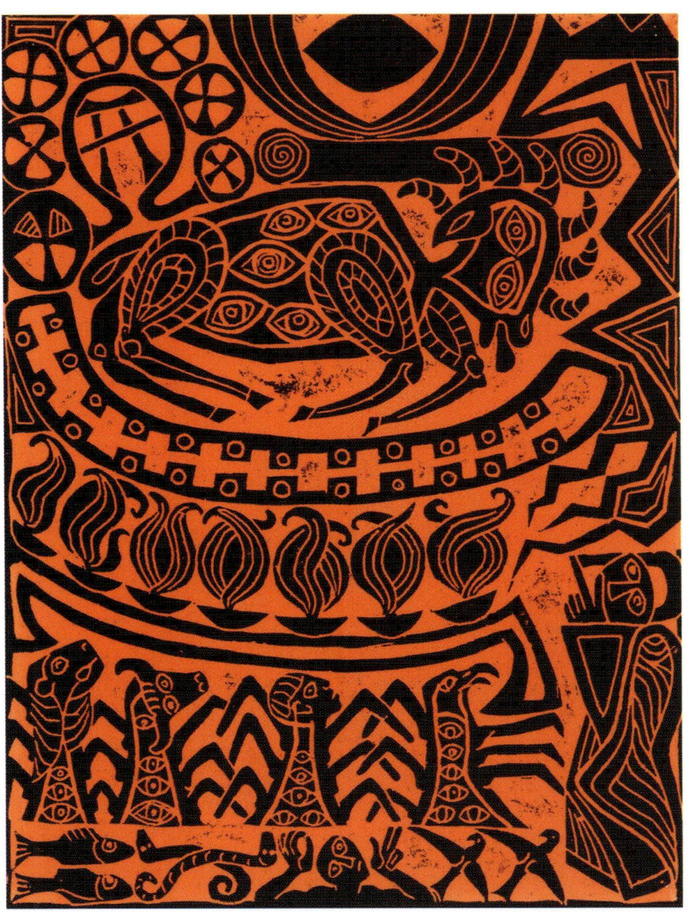

Johannes Offenbarung „Das Lamm mit den 7 Siegeln"
The Revelation of St John 'The Lamb with the 7 Seals'
1952, woodcut, 59 x 45 cm

Opposite: Egon Altdorf with a design for mosaic, c. 1952

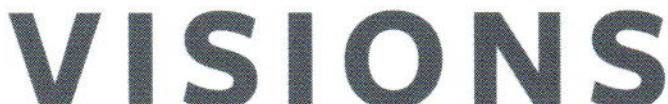

VISIONS

APOKALYPSE

In die Häupter schlagen die Dornen
der gewaltigen Reiter.

Treten die furchtbaren Hufe
auf die Leiber der Ungeborenen,
kälter werden die Augen
unter dem suchenden Helmrand.

Flammender Atem trifft höhnend
die ziehende Menge,
die ihren Strohwisch
tanzend umkreist.

Niemand erhört sie mehr.

Über dem Dampf
ihrer verseuchten Münder,
flieht das Gerechte
wie brennende Sonnen
und zeichnet sie klarer
in hilfloser Nacktheit.

Dome zerbersten,
in gewaltiger Scham
trifft sie der Fluch.

Unerbittlich zieht
und richtend,
glühende Lava,
mit dem lebenden Gott.

Meere verbrennen
an seinem Zorn,
gerichtet verdirbt,
wie die Fäulnis,
die Sonne.

APOCALYPSE

Thorns pierce the brows
of the mighty horsemen.

Their terrible hooves
trample the bodies of the unborn,
beneath the helmet's searching rim
the eyes grow colder.

Scornful, their fiery breath
licks at the surging crowd,
whose dance encircles
their scrap of straw.

No one hears them any more.

Above the miasma
of their defiled mouths,
righteousness flees
like burning suns,
brands them more surely
in their nakedness.

Cathedrals burst open,
stricken and cursed
in a torrent of shame.

Judicial, implacable,
lava moves,
a glowing tide
with the living God.

Oceans burn
in his wrath,
condemned and erased
like putrescence
in sunlight.

Johannes Offenbarung
„Die 4 Apokalyptischen Reiter"
The Revelation of St John 'The 4
Apocalyptic Riders'
1952, woodcut, 59 x 45 cm

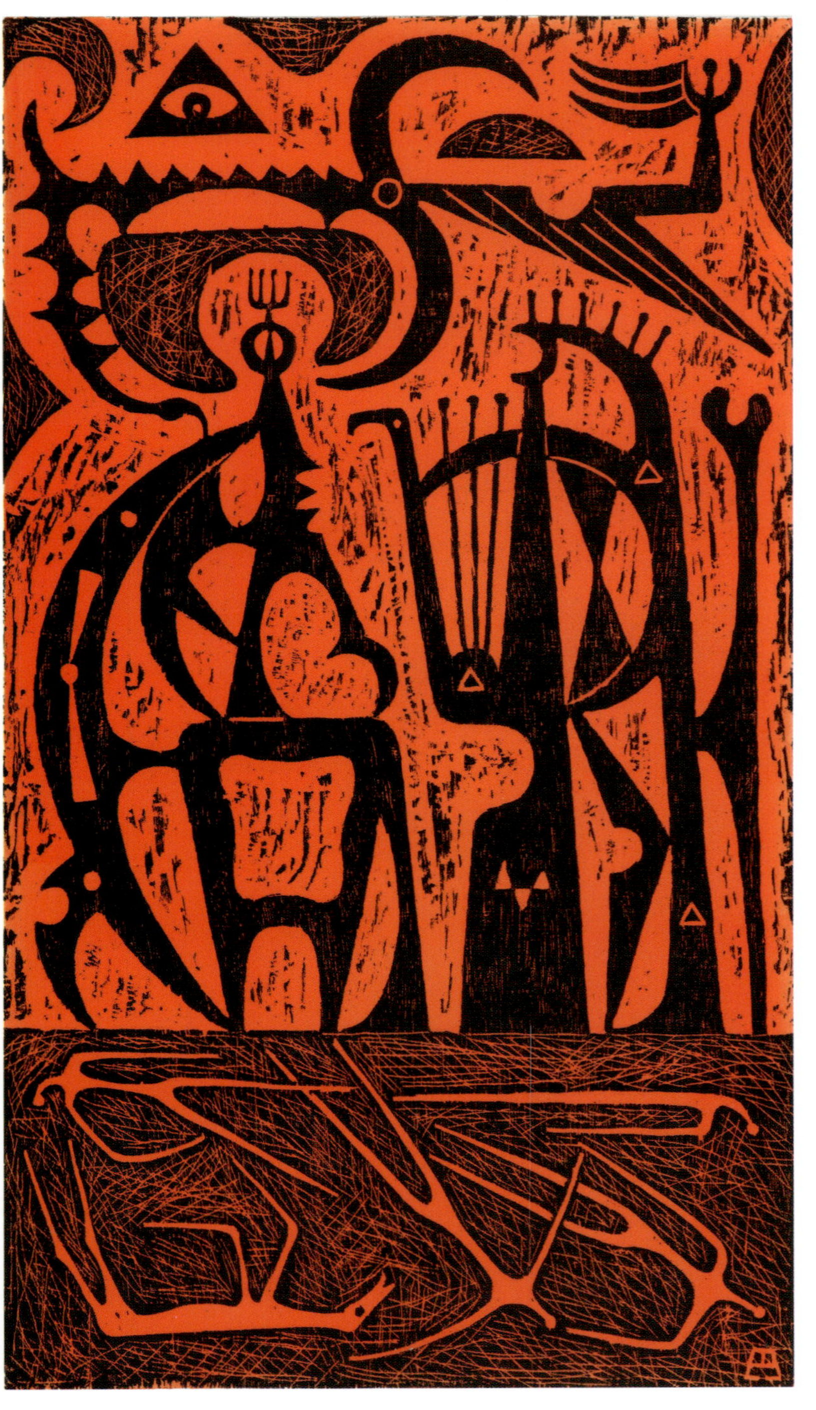

MADRIGAL

Spiel', Du Hand aus Mosaik,
auf der Harfe meiner Träume,
Flammenkreis aus sieben Mündern,
blaue Engel, rote Türme.

Schleier weht aus goldenen Haaren,
vielgestützter Thron aus Jade,
königliches Heer der Augen.

Stirnreif regenbogenfarbig,
Menschenaugenpaar erzittert,
über'm Firmament getragen,
schwebt die Streitmacht einer Schwurhand.

Eisenstarre schwarze Engel,
klirrend ihre Augenhärte,
tanzen, steingeflammte Schwerter
in dem Phosphorbrand der Hände.

MADRIGAL

Play, O thou mosaic hand
on the harp whereof I dream,
circle of flame from seven mouths,
angels blue, and towers red.

Golden hair and floating veil,
many footed throne of jade,
host of eyes to serve a king.

Circlet casting glints of rainbow,
dislocating human vision,
forces raised by sworn command
hover in the upper air.

Dance of black and iron-rigid
angels, clattering flinty eyes,
bearing stony flaming swords
in their phosphorous flare of hands.

David spielt vor Saul
David Plays before Saul
1955, woodcut, 60.5 x 35 cm

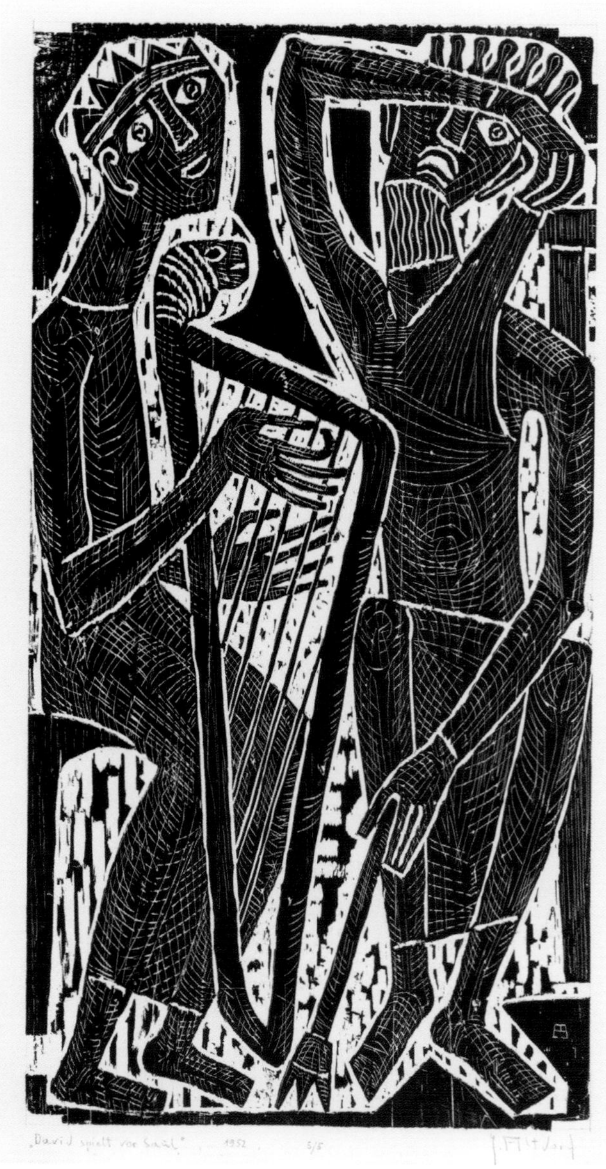

David spielt vor Saul
David Plays before Saul
1952, woodcut, 89 x 46 cm

DAVID SPIELT VOR SAUL

Umnachtet irrte Sauls Gehirn
in des Palastes weiten Räumen
und wühlte fiebernd in den Säumen
der schwarzen Wesen und im Nachtgestirn.

Auf seinem Thron verbrennt das Augenpaar,
die Hand verkrallt sich herrschend noch
auf goldenem Löwenhaupte, das ein Joch
der Furcht für seine Feinde war.

Geschnürt von seines Wahnsinns Schwüle
verwies er Menschen, welche kamen,
im Zorn verfluchte er heilige Namen
der Götter und versteinte sich in Kühle.

Als einst im eisigen Überschwang
das Furchtbare sein Haupt verhüllte,
vernahm er, wie ein fremder Klang
sein Ohr berührte und ganz füllte.

Das Zepter glitt aus seiner Hand,
die Augen blickten groß, und er erfaßte
das Bild des David, der da stand,
wie eine Sonne, die das Dunkel haßte.

Auf einer Harfe schwirrten reich die Saiten,
verwoben sich wie Sternenklang
und Weisheit fiel aus Ewigkeiten,
wie reife Früchte, aus dem Mund der sang.

Den König mächtig überspülte
Gewalt, die griff ihm stark ins Herze,
die Stirn brach auf und er erfühlte,
es floh wie ein Gespinst die Schwärze.

DAVID PLAYS BEFORE SAUL

Saul's tormented spirit ranged
across his palace's great rooms
and grubbed in its fever through the seams
of black creatures and among the stars.

Upon his throne two burning eyes,
a royal hand hooked in the golden mane
of the lion's head that was a yoke
of terror to his enemies.

Snared in the curdled air of madness
he cursed whoever crossed his path,
raged at the holy names of the gods
and turned in coldness into stone.

Till sunk one day in icy torpor,
the horror wound about his head,
he sensed a strange sound touch his ear
until it filled to overflowing.

Out of his hand the sceptre slipped,
his eyes grew wide, and beheld the vision
of David as he stood before him,
a shining sun that the darkness hated.

The shimmering strings of the harp wove
a rich cloth like the sound of stars,
and out of eternities wisdom fell
like ripe fruit from the singing mouth.

Violence like a breaking wave
overwhelmed the king and gripped his heart,
his brow broke open and he sensed
the darkness and the black webs flown.

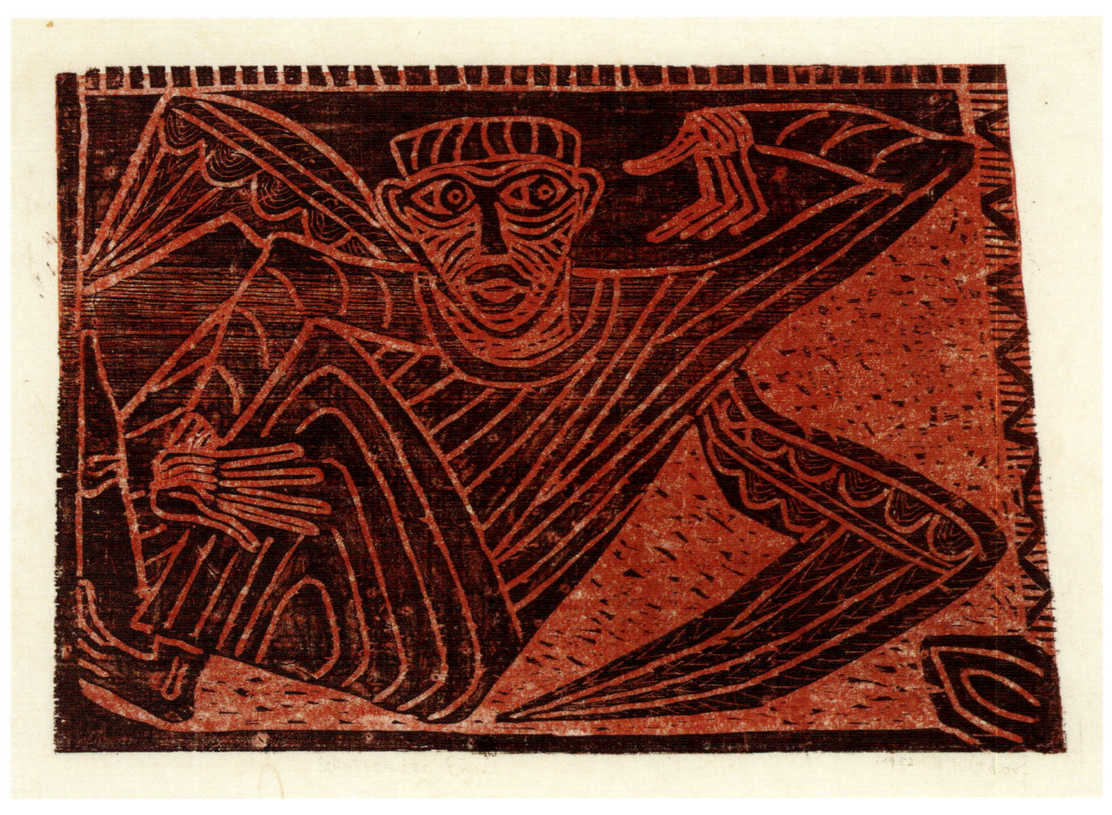

Stürzender Engel
Falling Angel
1952, woodcut, 43 x 64 cm

STÜRZENDER ENGEL

Als er verstoßen ward
und als er fiel,
begriff er
seine sinnlose Verschwendung,
er wollte anders sein.

In seinen Augen,
die sich langsam schlossen,
nahm er noch mit
den Bogen jenes Lichtes,
das ihn zum Kampf
erlesen hatte.

Die ihm gebotene Verheißung:
des Opfer sein,
des anders sein,
des Dunkel sein
zum ewigen Lichte.

Als er begriff,
war's letzte Liebestat:
er ließ sich fallen
in das ewige Dunkel.

FALLING ANGEL

Even as, cast out,
he fell,
he grasped
the senseless waste of him,
who had wanted to be other.

His eyes,
slowly closing,
yet gathered
the arc of that light
that had chosen him
for the battle.

The promise made to him:
to be sacrifice,
to be other,
to be darkness, set
against perpetual light.

Understanding it as
a final act of love,
he let himself fall
into perpetual darkness.

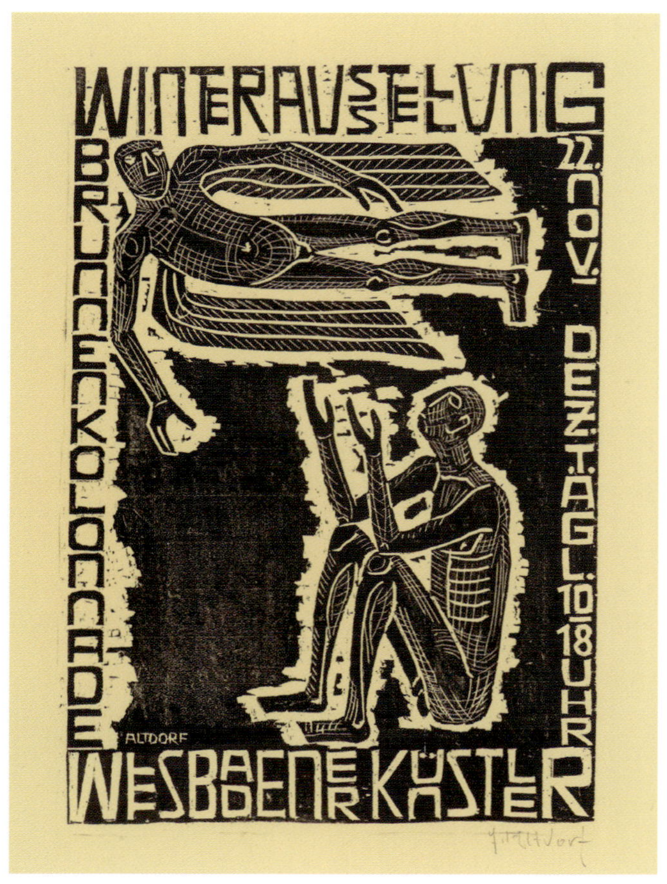

Poster for Winter Exhibition, Brunnen-Kolonnade, Wiesbaden
1952, woodcut, 42 x 40 cm

DER SCHWARZE ENGEL

Oh, du mein Engel,
im schwarzen Gewande
verbirgst du die Geißel
der menschlichen Qual
und all meine Tode.

Ist dir in deinen kristallenen Augen
der Milde so fremd,
wenn du mir erscheinst,
wie ein furchtbarer Fels?

Die menschliche Schuld
entflammt an der Macht
deines gierigen Schwertes.

Treff' mir ans Herz, du,
mit dem Groll deines Hasses:

Bin doch gemacht
aus lebendigem Stoff,
biegsam besing' ich
die Starrheit der Schwärze.

BLACK ANGEL

O you my Angel,
in your black robe
you hide the scourge
of human torment
and all my deaths.

Is kindness so strange
in your eyes of crystal,
in your terrifying presence
as sheer smooth stone?

Human guilt burns
before the might
of your eager sword.

Strike to my heart, Angel,
in your bitter hatred:

Yet made as I am
of living stuff,
pliant, I sing
unyielding blackness.

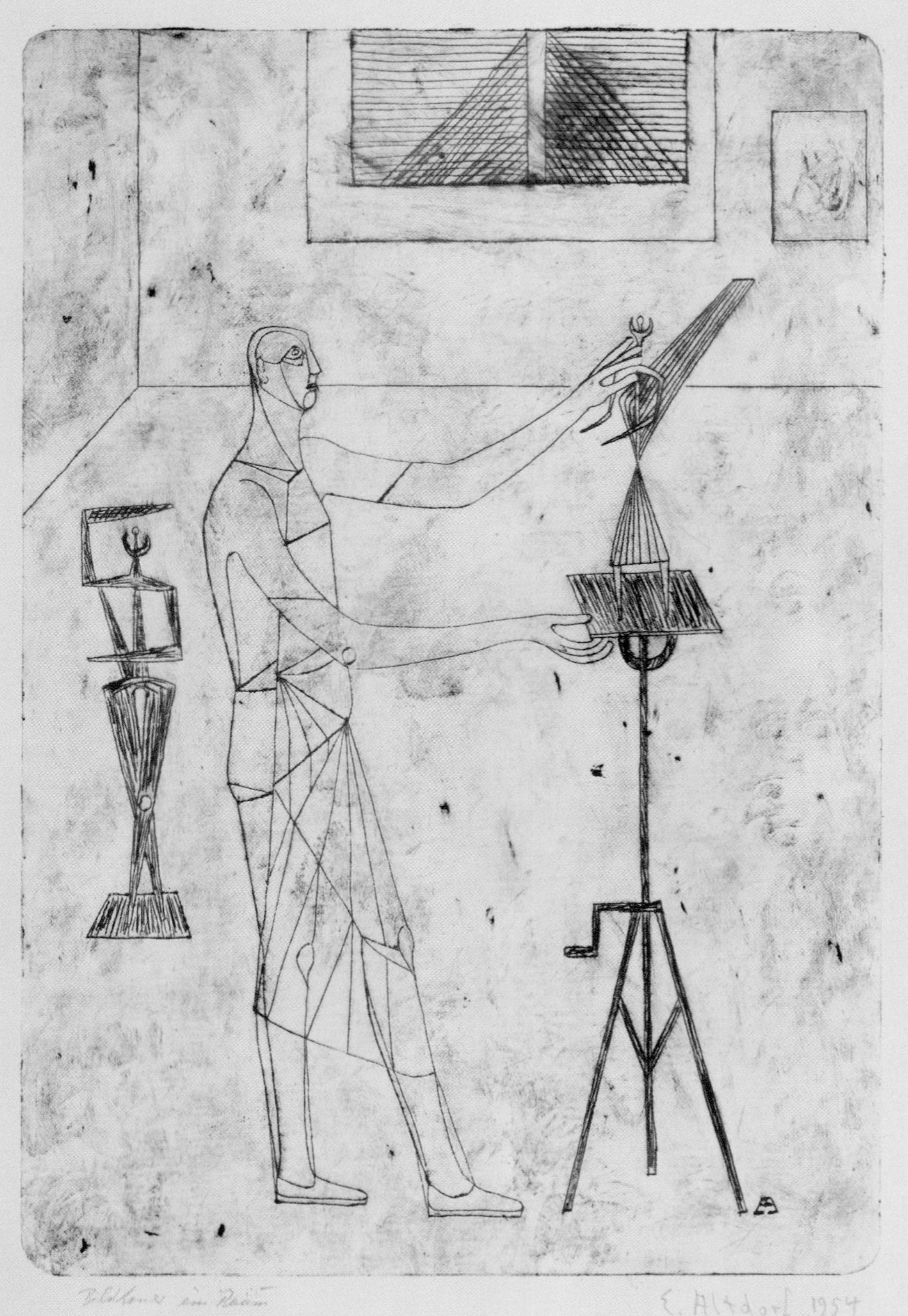

Bildhauer im Raum
Sculptor in the Studio
1954, etching, 40 x 28 cm

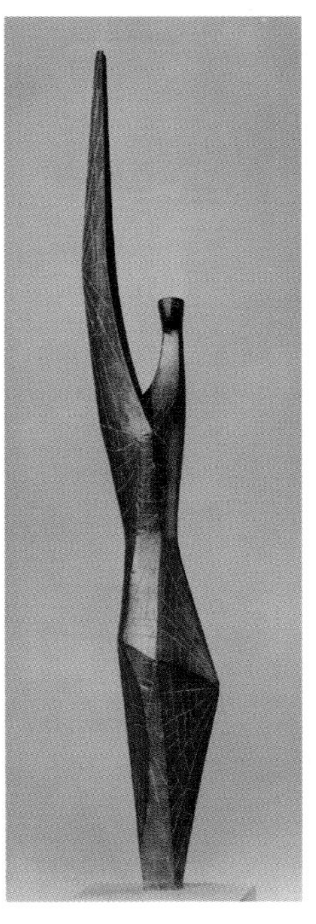

Nachricht
Message
1955, plaster, 60 cm (high),
untraced

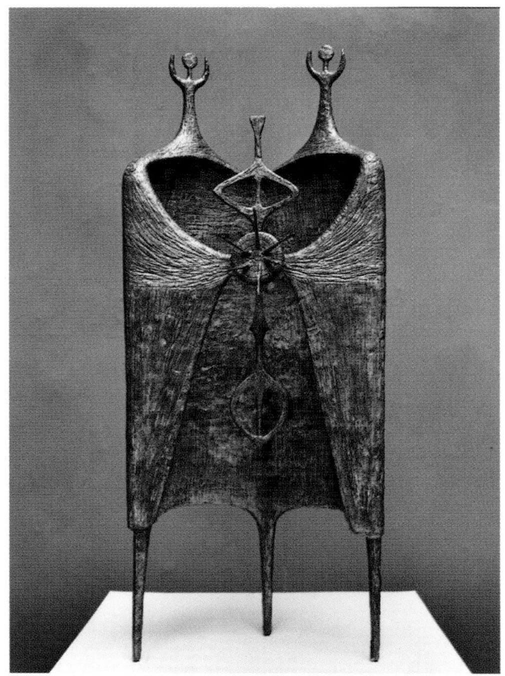

Wächter der Mitte
Guardian of the Middle
1955, plaster, 78 x 33 x 18 cm

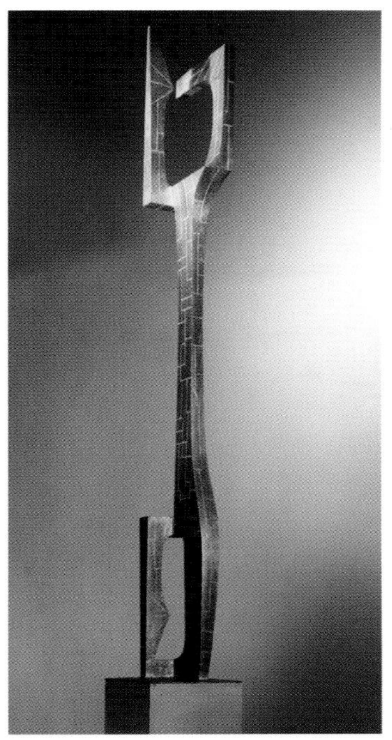

Modell für Fanal der Jugend
Model for Beacon of Youth
1960, painted plaster,
124 x 21 x 20 cm

TRANSFORMATION

FORMGEFÜHL 1946
Vom einem der auszog das Gruseln zu lernen

Beim Akt,
im Saal,
wird's jetzt fatal.

Es fällt die Hülle
man sieht kaum Fülle,
und ganz ohne Normen,
es schwanden die Formen,
steht müde und plun hungerig,
recht mager und plunderig,
zu aller Verdruss
die Neue Venus.

Den guten Rubens
er hätt es zerrissen,
er hätte auf die Kunstbeflissen
ein neues Formgefühl verwand.

Jedoch, man hällt Ideale offen,
und will auf bessere Zeiten hoffen,
es reizte stets ja das Verzwickte
Man rutscht recht häufig ins Abstricken . . .

SENSE OF FORM 1946
The story of one who set out to learn what fear is

That nude
in the hall,
is that it? is that all?

Out of her shell,
that poor girl looks like hell –
is this the new norm?
What happened to Fullness, or Form?
She's thin as a rake, a good feed's
what she needs –
The New Venus?
Give us a break.

Old Rubens,
he'd have known what to do:
Rip it up, bring a nice shiny new
Formgefühl to the party.

Well, you try to stick by your ideals,
and you hope better times come again,
the intricate always appeals,
you slide into a tangle of ends . . .

The German text is based on a typescript that is incomplete and often unclear. The wordplay in the poem sets up undercurrents and ambiguities of tone and meaning that are hard to preserve in translation. So in this case it's particularly true that the English version is only one of many possibilities.

The subtitle is a reference to the folk tale collected by the brothers Grimm.
Akt: has much the same senses as the English 'act', but can also mean, specifically, 'nude'.
ausziehen: to set out; to undress. *gruseln*: to get (or give someone) the creeps,
or a shiver of fear.

Egon Altdorf in his studio, c. 1952

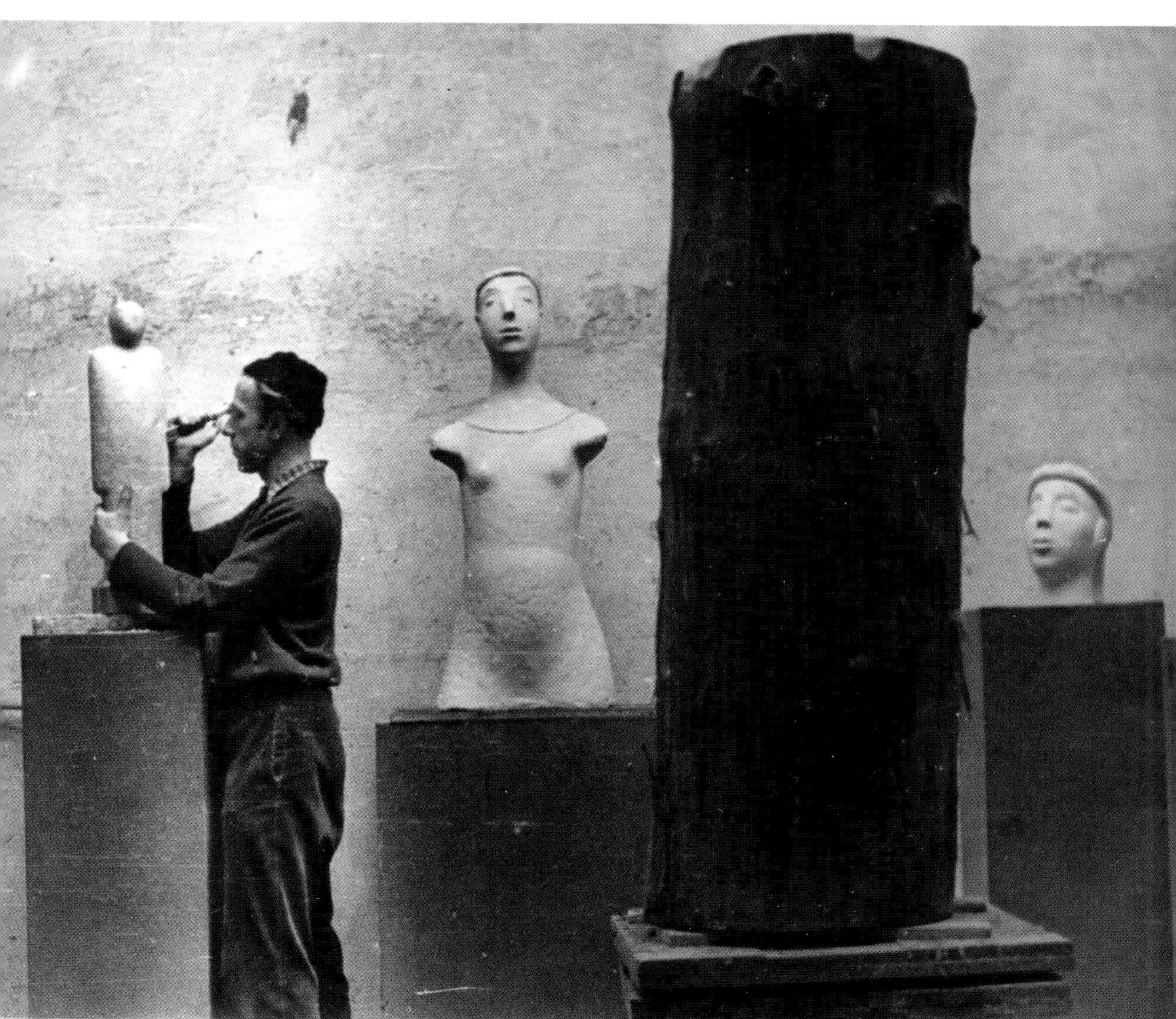

WANDLUNG

Das Blut der Baüme
ist mein Blut,
die Erde spiegelt
den Schlag meines Herzens.

Die Fächer der Wolken
sind meine Gedanken.

Das Aderngeflecht
der Wurzeln,
die wartenden Räume im Dunkeln
hauchen mich an.

Ich bin das Auge
des kristallinischen Vogels,
durch den die Welt fällt,
die Haut der Trommel,

die Höhlung der Muschel,
die tönende Stille,
das Geheimnis der Träume,
die atmende Liebe.

TRANSFORMATION

The blood of trees
is my blood,
the earth reflects
my beating heart.

The ranked clouds
are my thoughts.

The veiny network
of roots,
the spaces waiting in the darkness
breathe on me.

I am the eye
of the crystalline bird,
through which the world falls,
the skin of the drum,

the hollow of the shell,
the sounding stillness,
the mystery of dreams,
the breathing love.

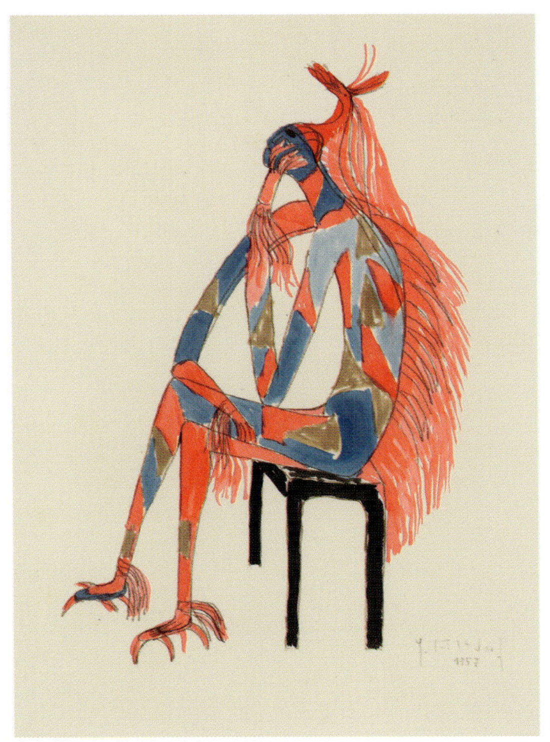

Firebird Dancer: costume design for Stravinsky's ballet
1957, ink and watercolour on paper, 52 x 38 cm

GOTISCHES BLATTWERK

Lobendes Blattwerk
aus Stein gehauen,
geschmeidiges Leben
in stiller Anbetung
über die Zeit.

Kapitelle, Trägerschaft
aufschwingender Bögen
zu schwebenden Sternenblüten.

Des Künstlers heiliger Wille,
die Demut seines Herzens,
die Sorgfalt
seiner führenden Hände.

Über Jahrhunderte,
wie noch anwesend,
berührt er mein Herz.

Ich fühle beglückt,
ich bin wie er
und spreche und wirke
aus gleichem Geiste.

Seht doch
aus kühlem Stein selbst
spricht die Liebe
zum Menschen
und das Lob der Welt.

Wir, die in stiller Schönheit
vor Gott
den Menschen rühmen.

CARVED GOTHIC FOLIAGE

Leafwork that praises
hewn out of stone,
a ripple of life
an adoration in stillness
across time.

Capitals, shafts that lift
arches that soar upwards
through weightless drifts of starflowers.

The artist's solemn will,
the submission in his heart,
the attentiveness
in his guiding hands.

Across the centuries,
as if still present,
he touches my heart.

I feel gifted with happiness
I am like him,
the same spirit
in what I do and say.

Yet see,
how out of the very stone
and its coolness, love speaks
to all of us,
and hymns the world.

We, who in unmoving beauty
before God
praise men and women.

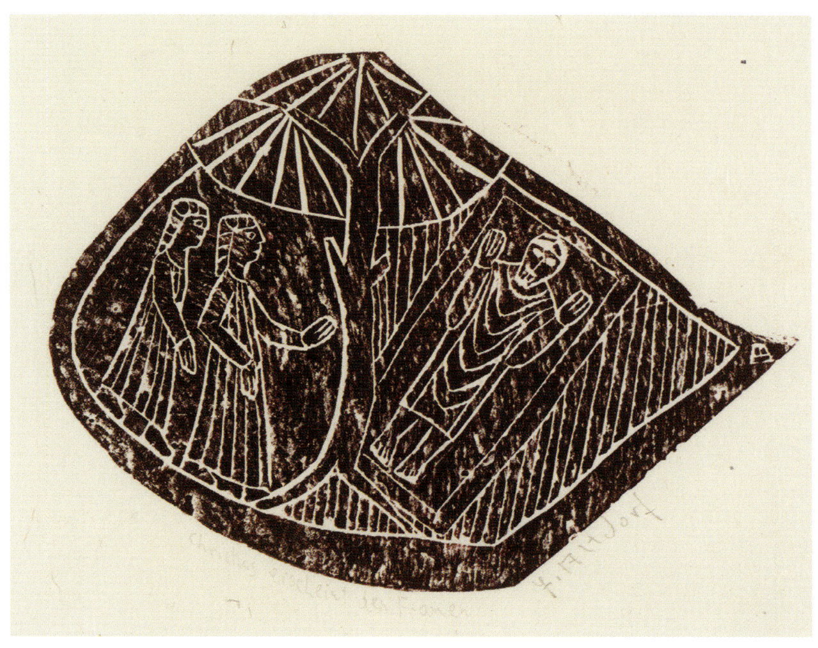

Christus erscheint den Frauen
Christ appears to the Women
1950, slate cut, 22 x 30 cm

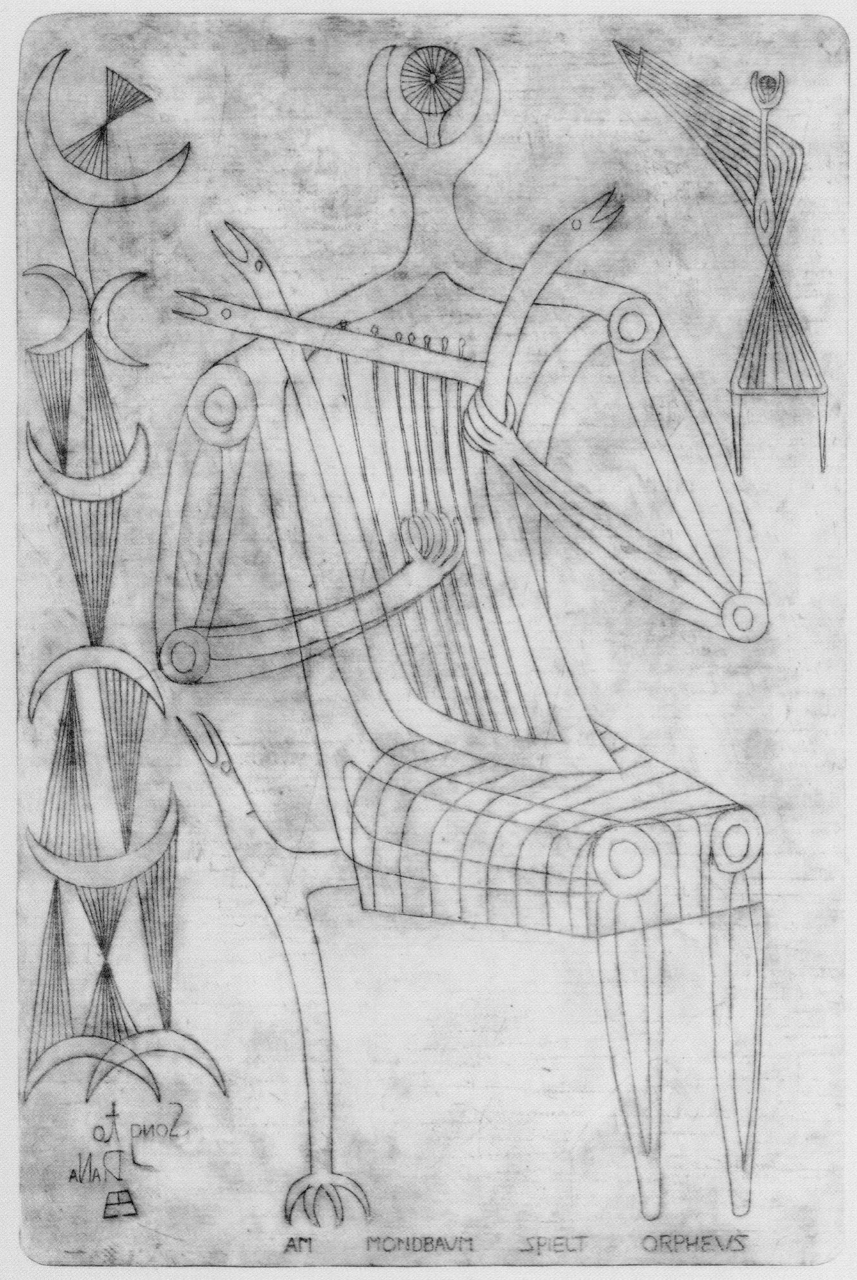
AM MONDBAUM SPIELT ORPHEVS

Am Mondbaum spielt Orpheus,
er opfert der Nacht
zerbrochene Sonnen unter den Füßen.

Aus Wurzeln der Monde,
Blüten verströmen
im wartenden Dunkel
phosphorene Sterne.

Die täglichen Hände,
verbrannt am Geflecht
verloschener Sonnen,
fügten die nächtlichen Tiere zur Harfe.

Im Fieber der Hände,
mit blinden Augen
zerteilt er das Dunkel.

Der Hauch seines Mundes,
in grabfeuchtem Nebel,
formt sich im Spiele
die Schemen des Traumes.

Orpheus plays beside the moon-tree,
he offers to the night
broken suns underfoot.

From the roots of moons,
in the waiting darkness
from blossoms stream
phosphorescent stars.

Diurnal hands,
seared at the web
of burnt-out suns,
fused nocturnal animals to the harp.

With fevered hands,
blind eyed
he parts the darkness.

The breath from his mouth
in the dank fog of graves
forms as it plays
the dream's spectral patterns.

Am Mondbaum spielt Orpheus
Orpheus Plays beside the Moon-Tree
1953, etching, 60 x 40 cm

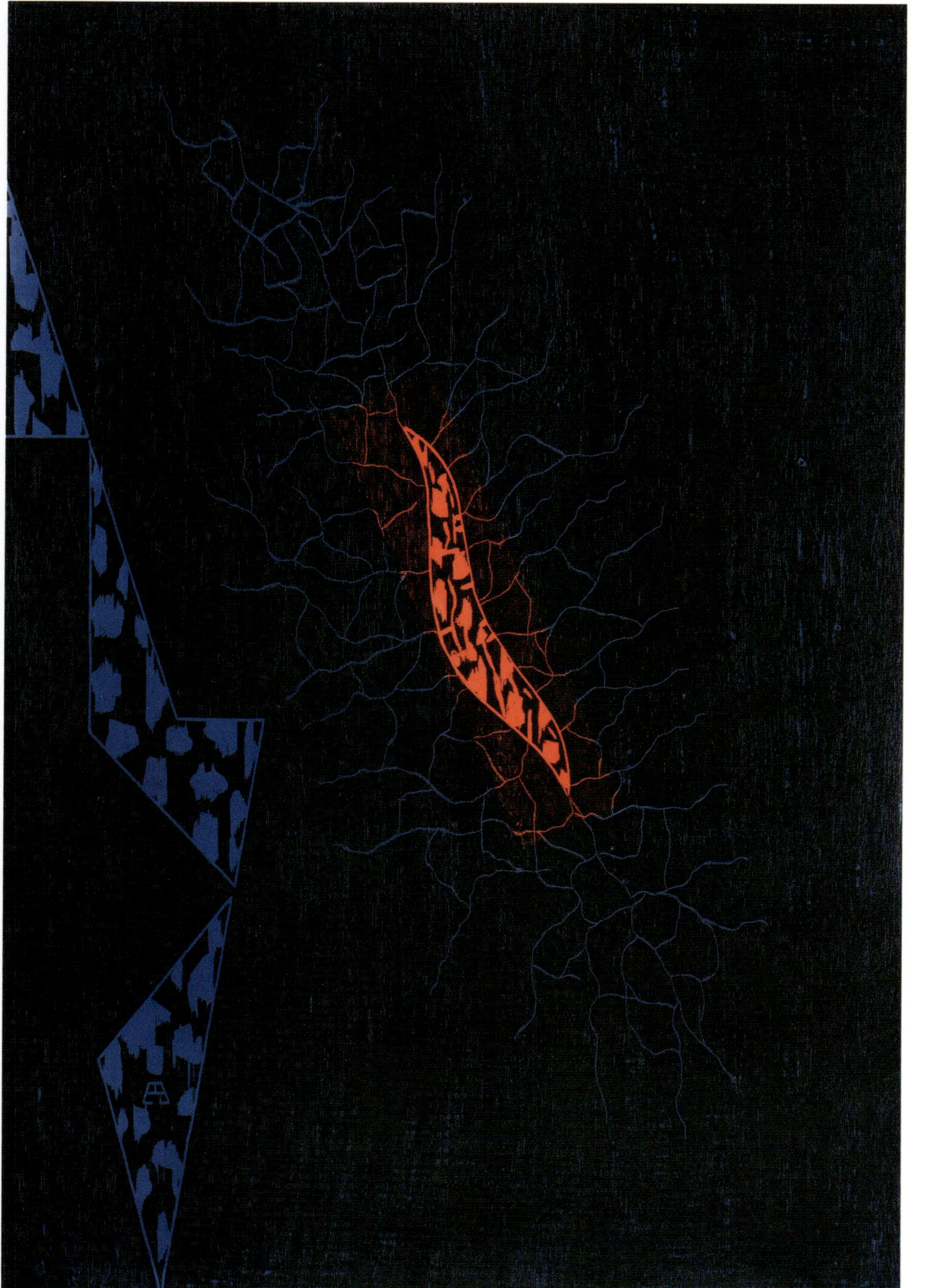

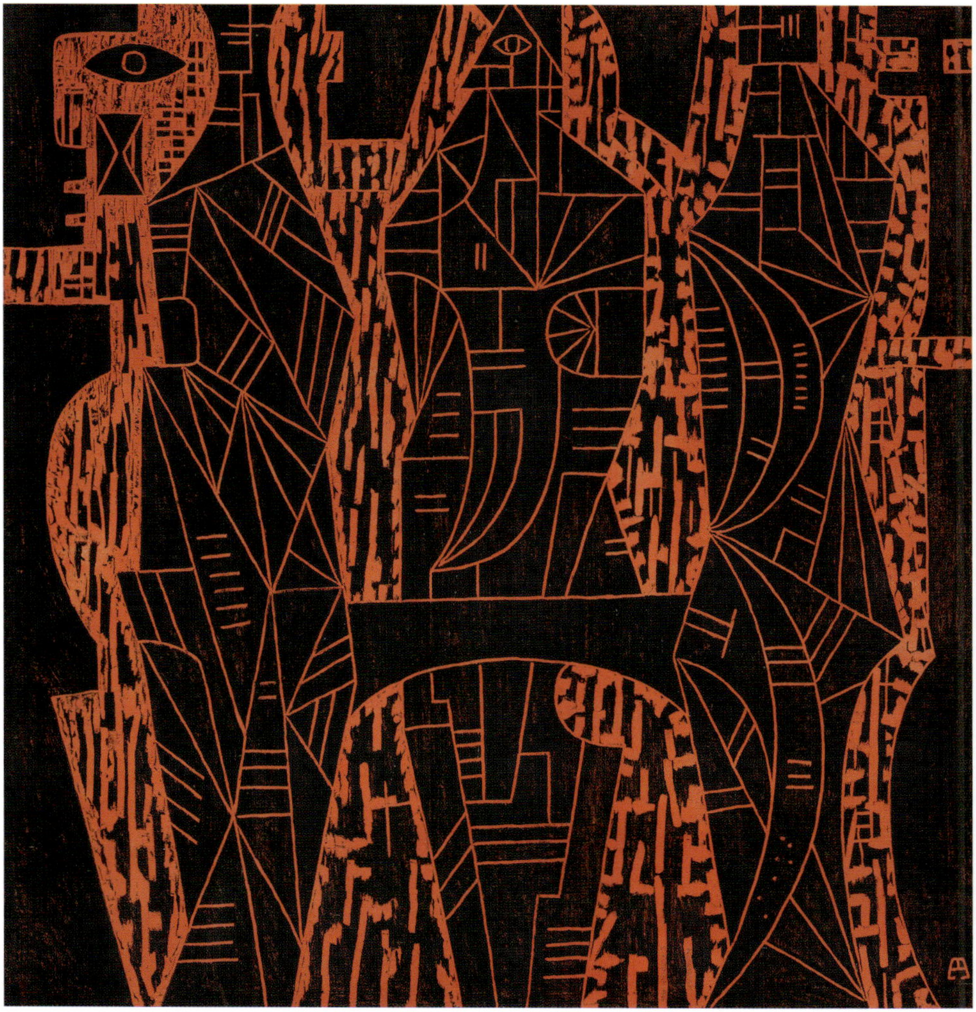

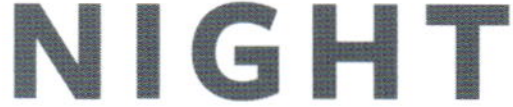

Korrespondenz
Correspondence
1957, woodcut, 120 x 120 cm

Opposite: Nächtliche Wunde
Nocturnal Wound
1964, woodcut, 85 x 60 cm

NIGHT

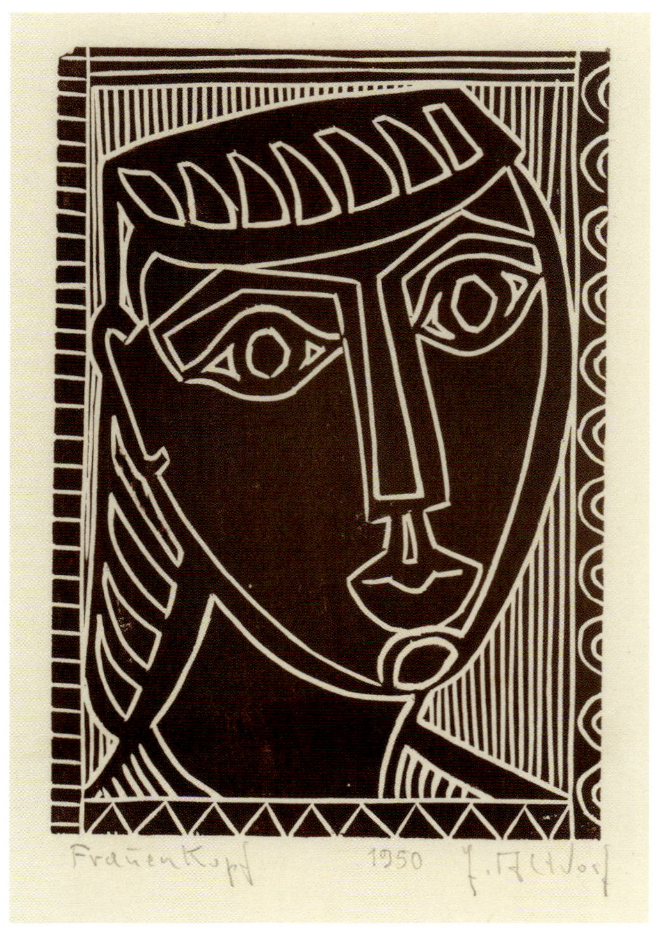

Frauenkopf
Woman's Head
1950, woodcut, 24.4 x 17 cm

ORPHEUS

Die Weiße des Fußes
wurde sein Auge,
Geschicke verbargen
die Male des Weges.

Durch zeitlose Nächte
schwarzer Gebilde
spielt ihn der Tanz
gestoßen vom Traum.

Ein Wesen zeichnet
auf den Rücken des Mantels,
für Augen verborgen,
siebenfache Gesetze.

Gebannt in die Hände,
tastet sich vor,
die suchende Stimme.

Bei ihrem Klange
schwinden die Brücken,
Treppen zerfließen
unter schwebendem Fuß.

Die Wesen des Dunkel
flechten die Kette,
im Schwung seines Ganges:
Eurydike.

ORPHEUS

The whiteness of the foot
became his eye,
fates hid
what marked the path.

Through timeless nights
of black imaginings
and hurt by the dream
the dance plays him.

A creature marks
the back of his cloak,
sevenfold laws,
withheld from sight.

Spelled into his hands,
the searching voice
feels its way forward.

At its music
bridges dissolve,
stairs melt away
under the hesitant foot.

Creatures of the dark
weave the chain,
in time with his step:
Eurydice.

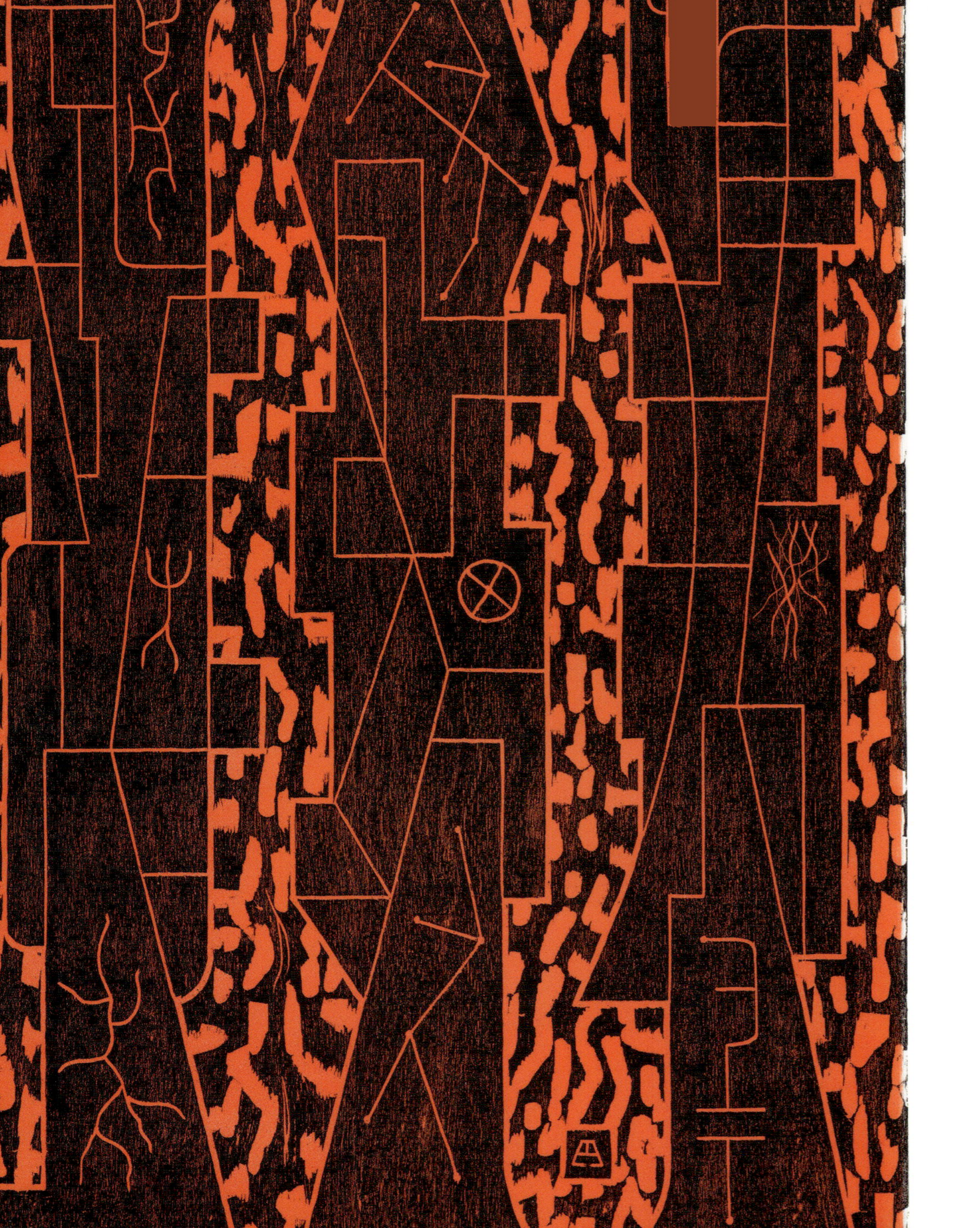

MAGIE

Die nasse Haut
des schwarzen Asphalt
verwandelt die Straßen
und alle sind gleich.

Vor Irrlichtern flüchten,
in Labyrinthen,
die Schatten der Wesen
wie flüchtiges Spiel.

In traumlosem Dunkel
flechten sie Kränze
von glitzernden Perlen
und schütten sie aus.

MAGIC

The wet skin
of the black asphalt
transforms the streets
and all are alike.

Shadows of creatures
are chased through labyrinths
by will o'the wisps,
like a fleeting game.

In dreamless darkness
they fashion garlands
of glistening pearls,
then let them spill.

Drei kosmische Stelen
Three Cosmic Stelae
1963, woodcut, 84.5 x 60 cm

Zur Mondnacht,
wenn die Stille sich krönt,
unter der uralten Kiefer,

führt Tau und Traum,
silbern verwoben,
brüderlich,
den schweigsamen König.

Mit ihrer kühlen Sternenpracht
besiegt die Nacht den Tag,

erlösend zieht durch uns die Ruh'
und wiegt,

im Duft der feuchten Erde,
uns in die Allmacht Schlaf,

aus der wir kamen.

By moonlight,
when the stillness crowns itself
under the ageless pines,

Dew and Dream,
woven together in silver,
like brothers
lead the silent king.

Night in her cool starry splendour
overcomes day.

Quietness redeems and runs through us,
cradles us

in the scent of the wet earth,
lulls us into the great sleep,

from which we came.

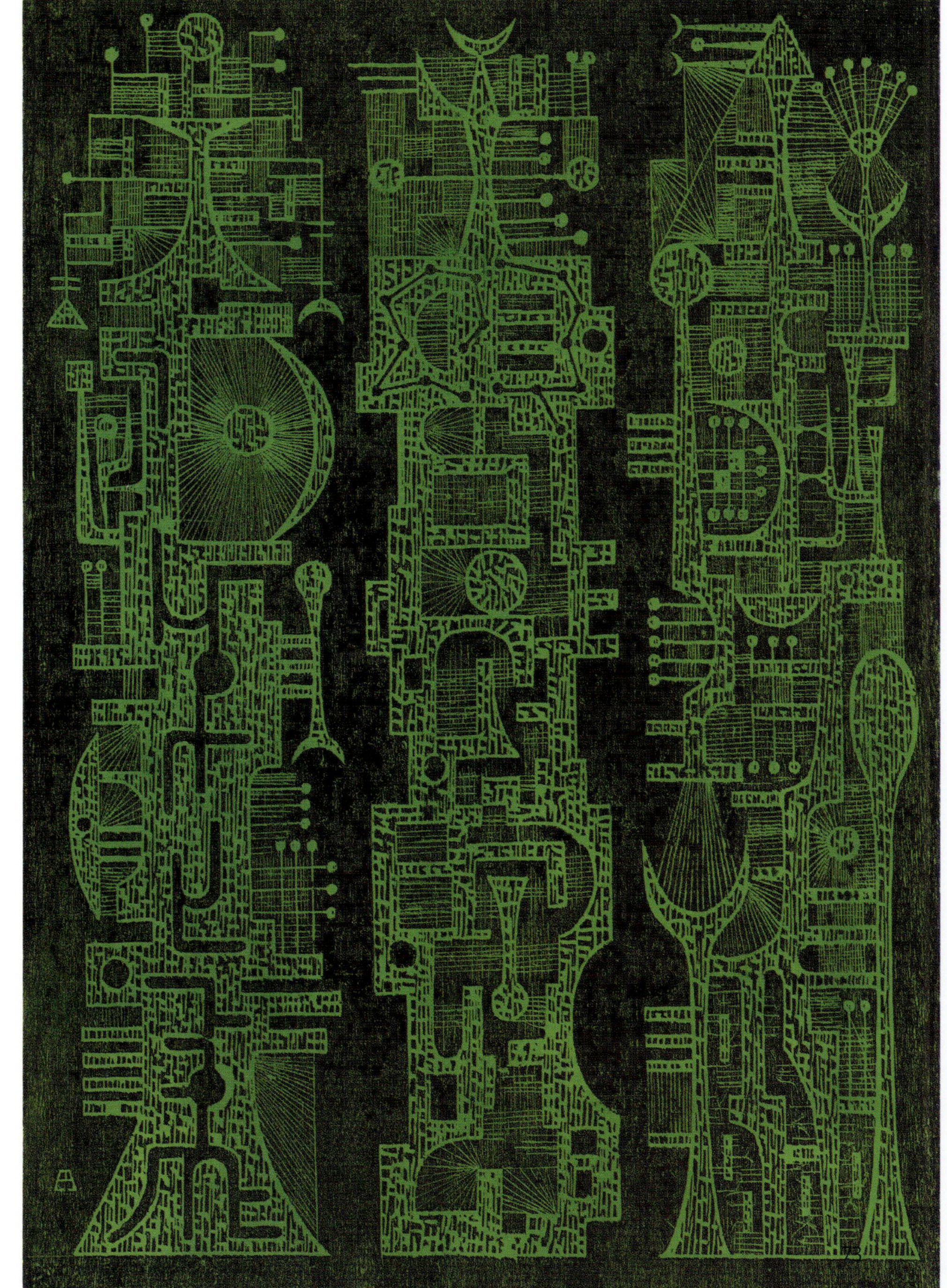

Traum der Könige
Dream of the Kings
1956, woodcut,
84.5 x 60 cm

KINDER DES PFLUGES
Zur Skulptur „Pflugfigur" von Egon Altdorf

Wir Kinder des Pfluges,
die mit nächtlichem Tasten
die Hand an das Himmelsspiel legen.

Unser kindliches Herz,
das liebt,
das Geheimnisse singt.

Durch uns geht der Pflug
und die goldene Scheibe,
die nachts, wenn die Welt schläft,
ihren Traum wacht und deutet.

In dem nachtblauen Mantel,
in dem mondkalten Silber,
seine atmenden Flügel
ziehen durch unsere Träume.

Nachts singt der Pflug
seinen glühenden Erztraum,
vom Beginn der Erde,
vom verwandelnden Feuer,

sein Mund tönt mächtig,
wie die Kupferpauke des Himmels.

CHILDREN OF THE PLOUGH
After the sculpture 'Plough-Figure' by Egon Altdorf

We children of the plough,
who with hesitant, nocturnal hands
play the sky game.

Our childlike hearts
that love
sing the mystery.

The plough passes through us,
and the golden disc,
which at night, while the world is asleep and dreaming,
watches and interprets.

in the night-blue mantle,
in the moon-cold silver,
its breathing wings
beat through our dreams.

At night the plough sings
its dream of glowing ore,
from the earth's beginning,
from the transforming fire,

its mouth resounds
like the copper drum of the sky.

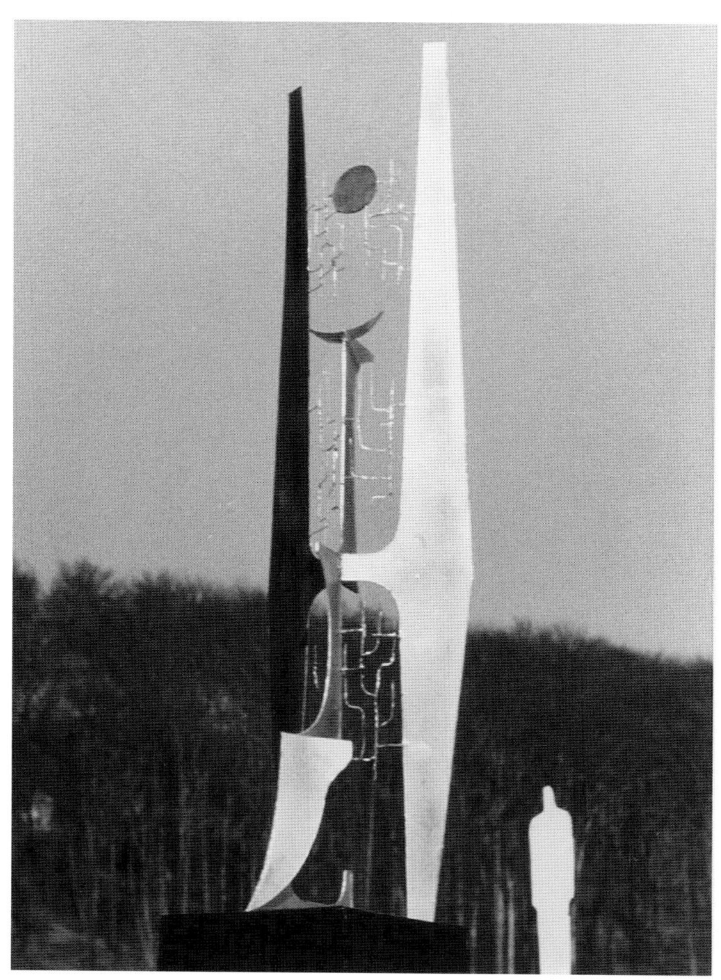

Pflugfigur
Plough-Figure
1959, cardboard, 60 cm (high)

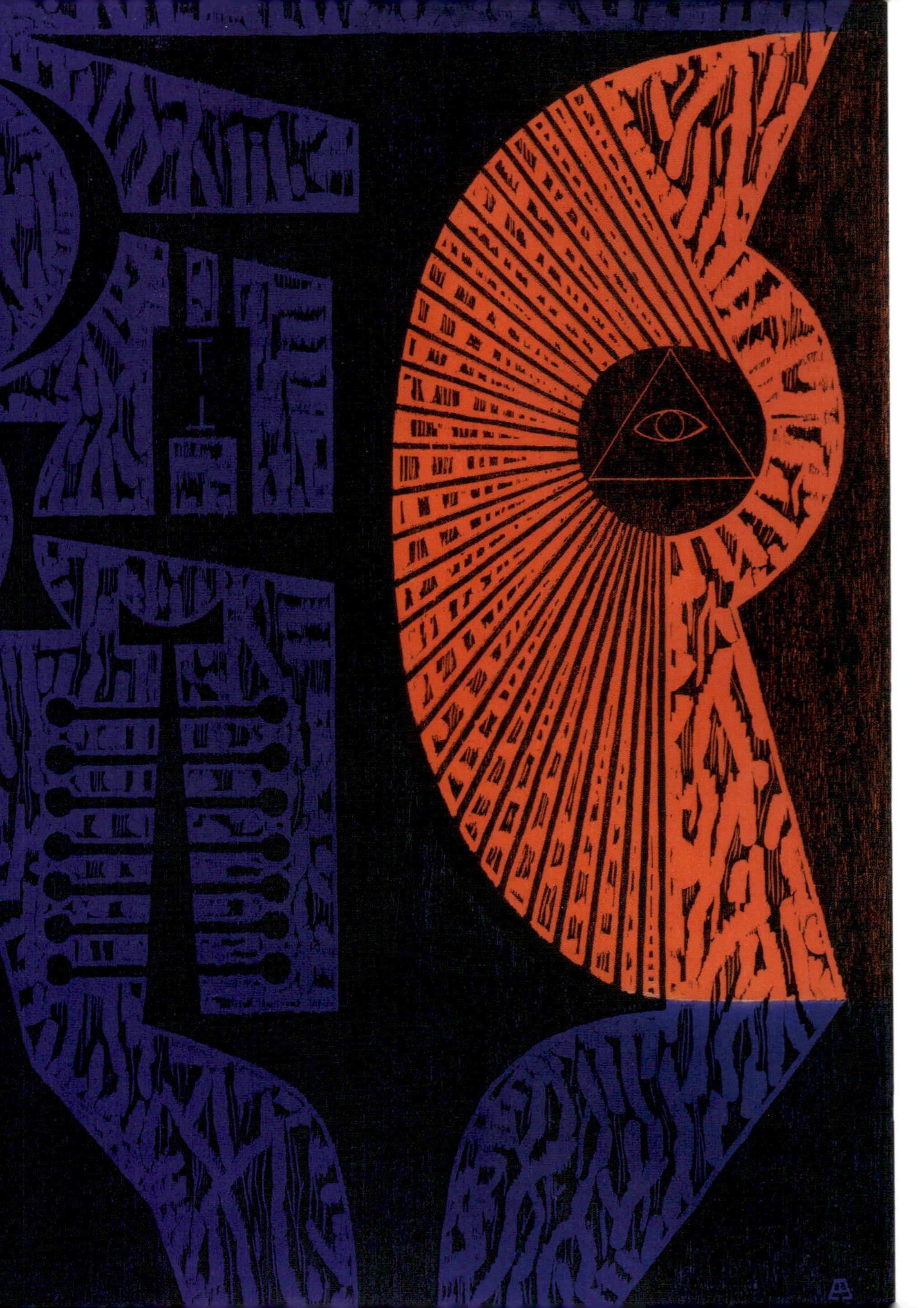

NÄCHTLICHER BOTE

Du nächtlicher Bote,
ich finde deine Zeichen,

in der Weite des Himmels,
in dem Wachstum der Bäume,
in den Gesichtern der Menschen,
in den Augen der Tiere.

Mit staunenden Augen,
mit schweigendem Munde
folg ich der Vielzahl
deiner Gesetze.

Die magische Dunkelheit saugt mich an.

Die Atmung der Toten
wird meine Würde,
das tonlose Nichts
wird mein Spiegel.

In meine Augen fällt die Welt.

Der bebende Stoff
der lebenden Atmung
formt meine Sehnsucht
und folgt meinem Traum.

NOCTURNAL MESSENGER

Nocturnal messenger,
I find your signs

in the vastness of the heavens,
in the growth of trees,
in the faces of men and women,
in the eyes of animals.

With wondering eyes,
with silent mouth
I trace the manifold
of your laws.

The magical darkness sucks me in.

The breathing of the dead
becomes my dignity,
the soundless void
my mirror.

The world falls into my eyes.

The trembling stuff
of living breath
shapes my longing,
follows my dream.

Kopfidol mit Scheibe, Mondzeichen, Stundenglaszeichen und Kronenzeichen
Head-Idol with Disc, Moon-Sign, Hourglass-Sign and Crown-Sign
1957, woodcut, 84.5 x 60 cm

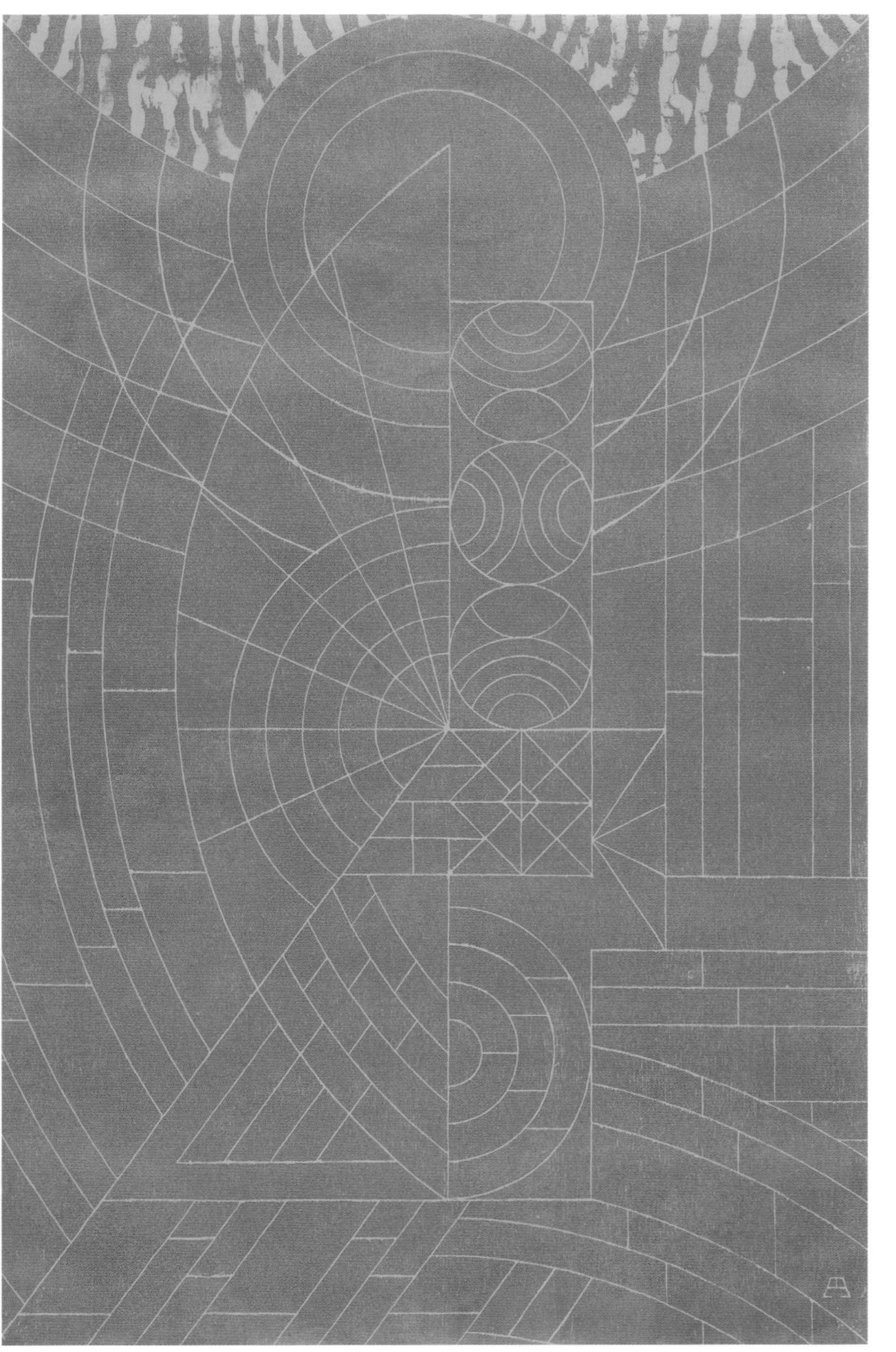

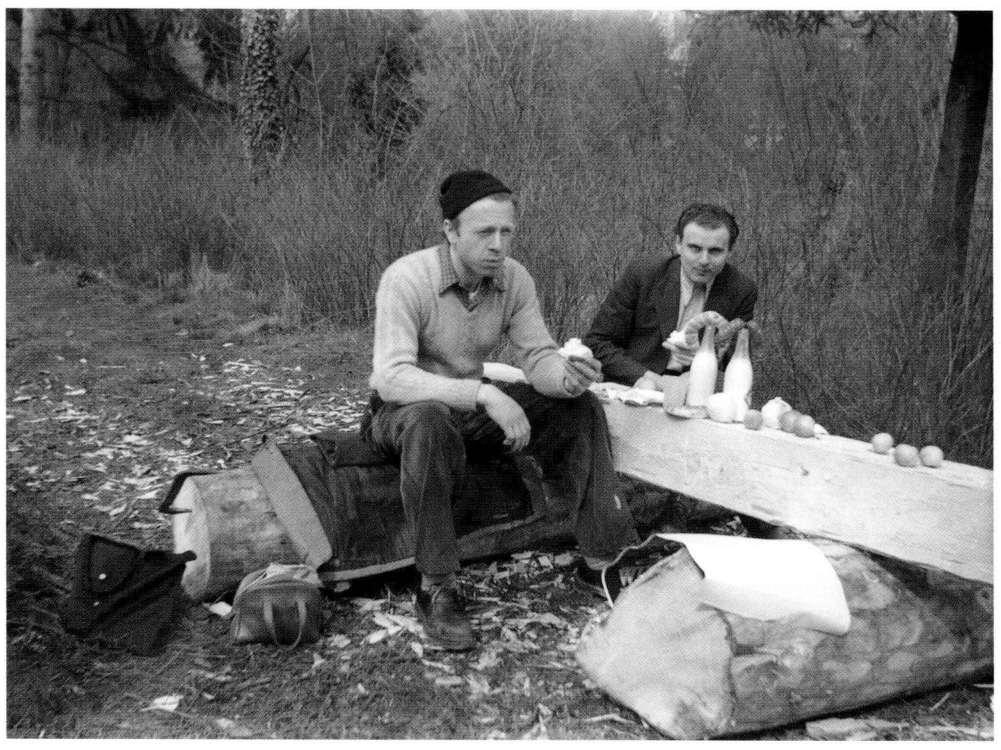

Egon Altdorf with unknown companion, c. 1952

Opposite: **Una Terra Sancta: Gespräch mit der Erde (Keimform)**
Una Terra Sancta: Conversation with the Earth (Seed Form)
1998, wocdcut, 90.5 x 60 cm

SEASONS

DIE SPRACHE DER ROTEN ÄPFEL

Von weit schon grüßend
leuchtet die freudige Sprache
der roten Äpfel.

Wir schauen in die Wunderspiegel
der herbstlichen Zeit.

Uns hebt die klare Weite,
wir werden getragen
von der kühlen Atmung
des reinen Lichtes.

Wir fühlen beglückt
die strömende Gnade
des Lebens
und die gewährte Zeit.

THE LANGUAGE OF RED APPLES

Greeting you from afar,
it glows, the joyous language
of red apples.

We look into the miraculous mirror
of autumn time.

The clear distance lifts us,
we are borne along
by the cool breathing
of pure light.

We feel gifted with happiness
the streaming grace
of life
and the time granted to us.

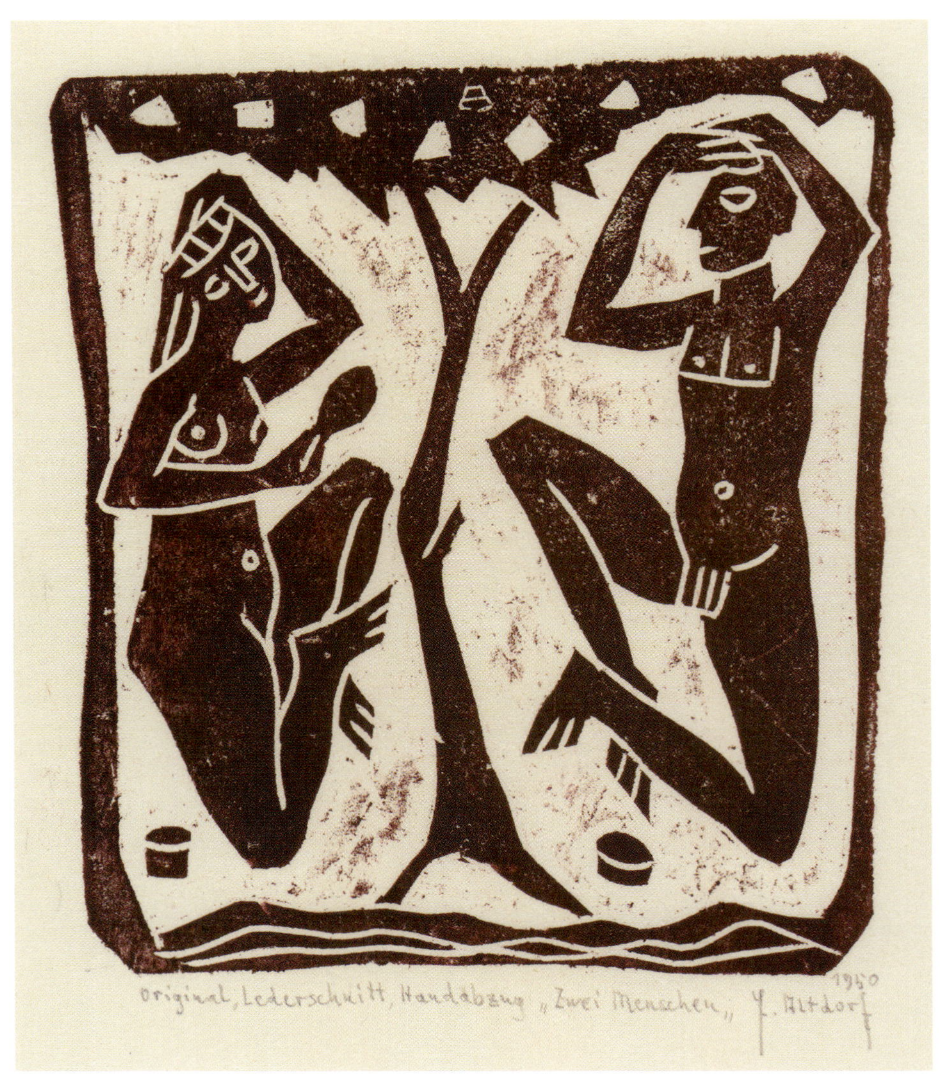

Zwei Menschen
Two Figures
1950, leathercut, 19.5 x 18 cm

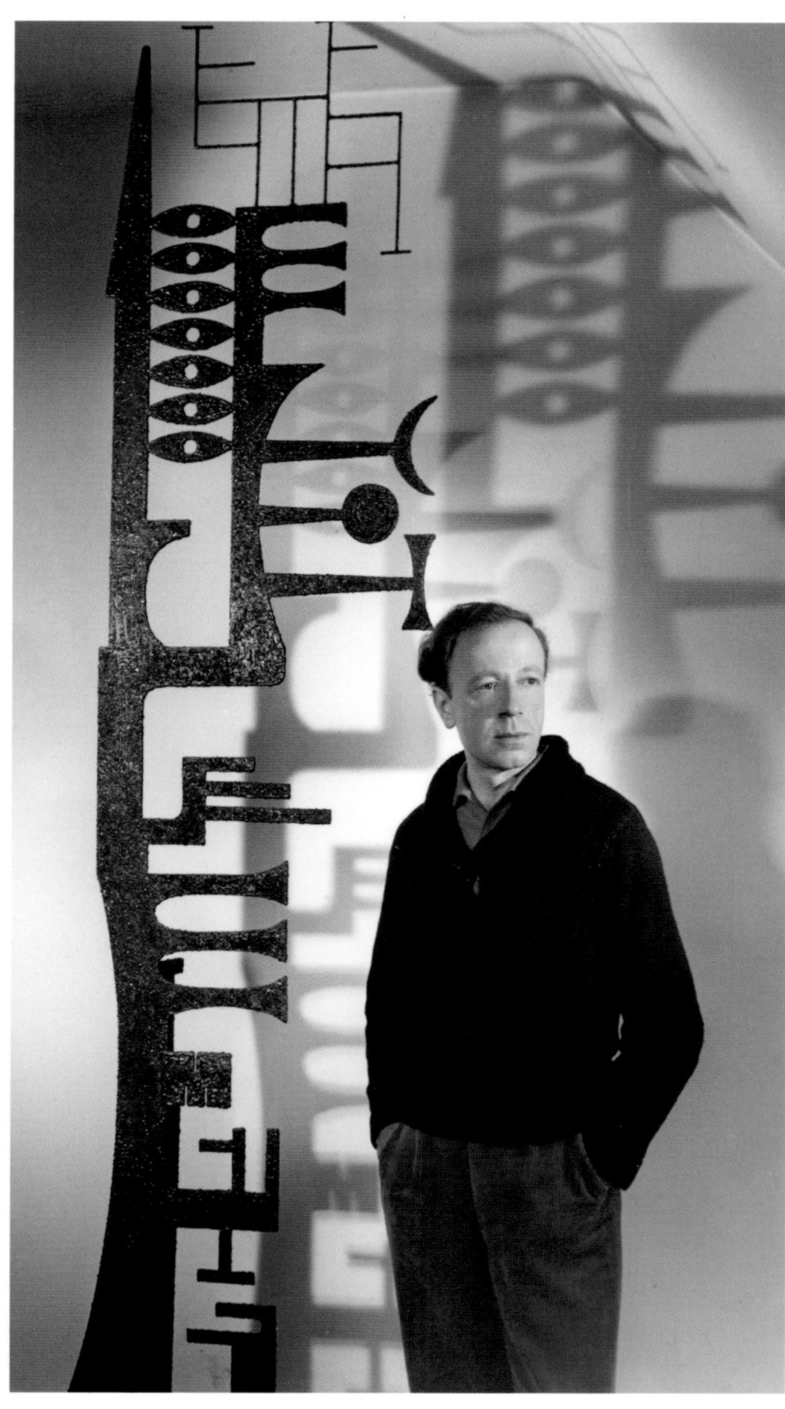

Egon Altdorf mit „Pflugfigur mit 7 Augen und Kronenmotiv", 1960
Egon Altdorf with *Plough-Figure with 7 Eyes and Crown-Motif*, 1960

DIE ZEIT DER FALLENDEN BLÄTTER

Es beginnt die Zeit
der fallenden Blätter.

Die gepflügten Äcker
wölben sich wieder
mit ihrer wartenden Erde
in die Bläue des Himmels.

Sie tauchen
in die wandernde Sprache
mächtiger Wolkengebirge,
die silberweiß thronen.

Nun Schweigen die Pflüge,
sie haben mit der Erde gesprochen,
sie haben die Erde gewendet
in ihrem Geheimnis.

THE TIME OF FALLING LEAVES

Now begins the time
of falling leaves.

The ploughed fields
with their waiting earth
arch their backs again
into the blue of heaven.

They rise
into the wandering language
of majestic cloud formations,
throned in silver-white.

Now the ploughs are silent,
they have spoken with the earth,
they have turned the earth
in their mystery.

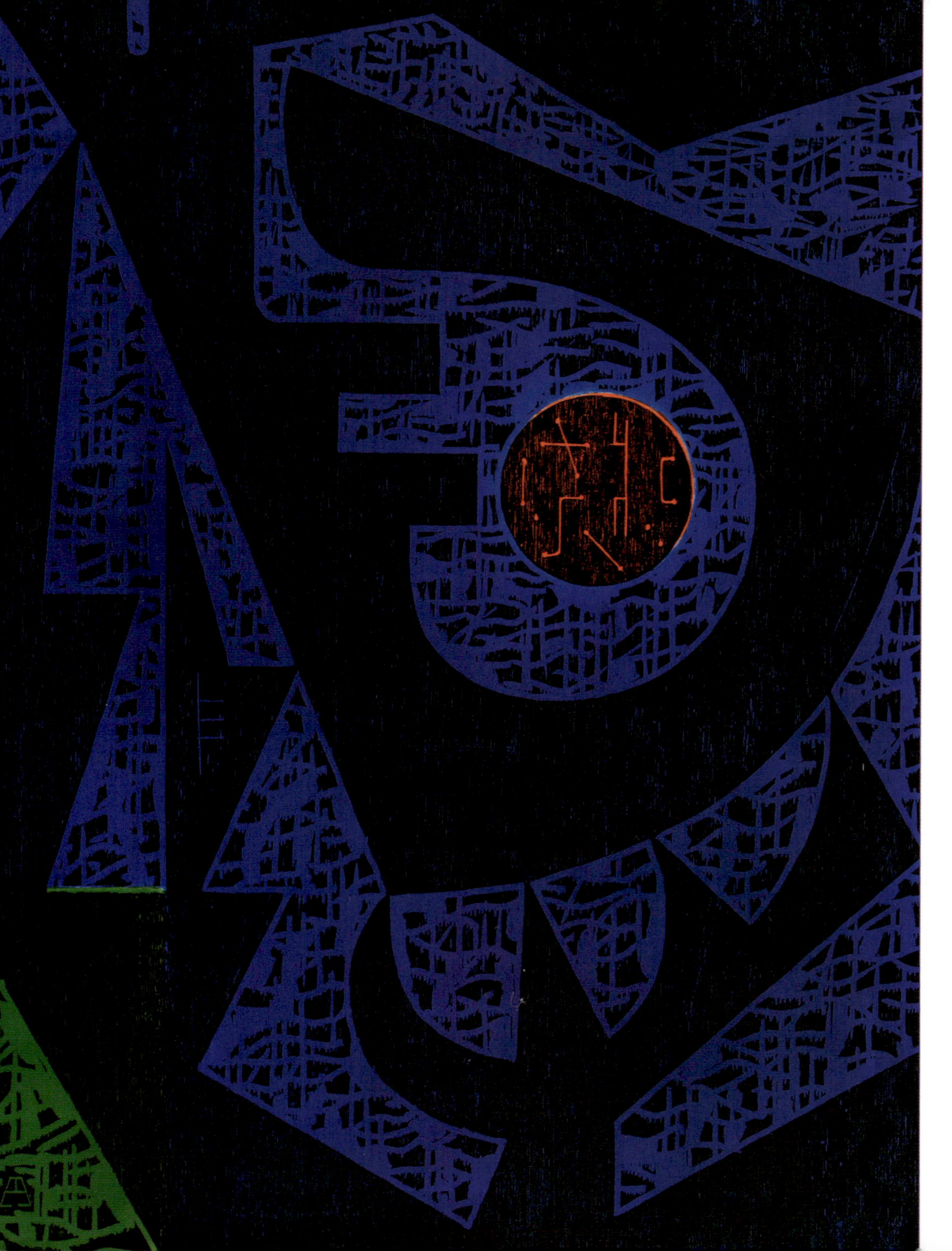

HERBST

Der Holunder verblutet
in dunkelen Gebüschen,

des Nachts,
wenn niemand sie verspürt,
verkühlen sommerwarme Winde
in grauen wartenden Feldern.

Wie unendlich waren die Nächte,
wie groß und schwer die Gestirne,
wie unersättlich war und trunken,
mein kleines menschliches Lied.

AUTUMN

The elder bleeds away
in dark thickets,

at night,
when no one feels them,
warm summer winds grow chill
in grey waiting fields.

How endless were the nights,
how great and heavy the stars,
how unslakeable and drunken,
my small human song.

Kampf der Elemente
Battle of the Elements
1963, woodcut, 80.5 x 60.5 cm

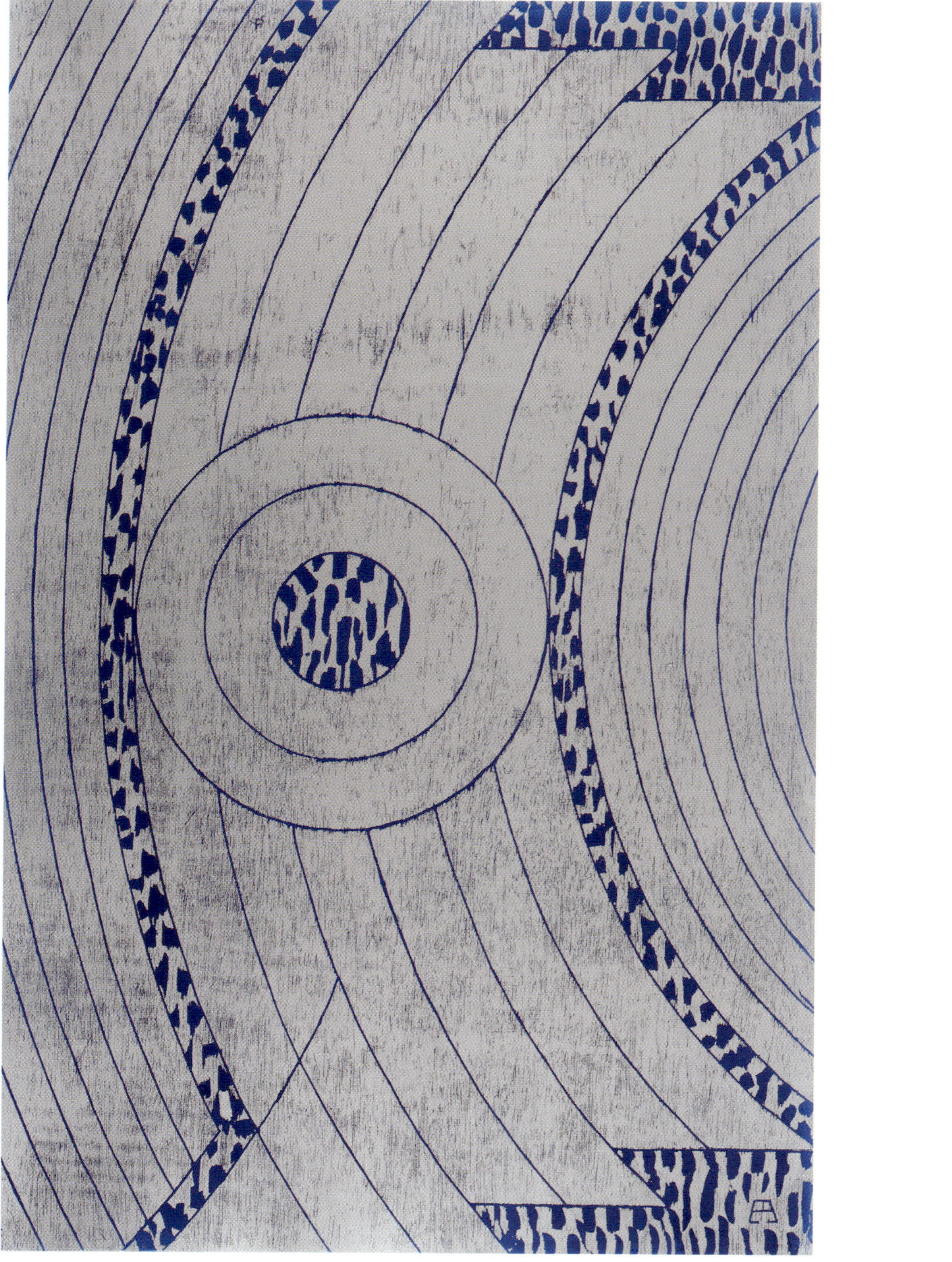

In regennassen Alleen
ertasten die Gehenden
mit einsamen Händen
ihre verlorenen Träume.

Als sichtbares Spiel
verwandelt der Engel
wartend und gültig
das modernde Laub.

Wie glitzernde Schreine
an frühen Gräbern
stehen die Bäume
feucht übertränt.

In rain-soaked avenues
walkers feel
their lost dreams
with lonely hands.

As a visible game
the angel transforms
with patience and reason
the rotting foliage.

Like the glistening shrines
of early graves,
the trees stand
drenched and streaming.

Flügel des Regens
Rain Wing
1979, woodcut, 90.5 x 60 cm

In dem fallenden Schnee
der gefiederten Blüten
schweben Ewigkeiten
und die atmende Zeit.

Wie tonlos geflüstertes
Amen der Toten.
Und die stille Hoffnung
der Liebe,
der Traum der Lebenden.

Der stille Mund des Lebens
gibt kein Geheimnis preis,
er verwandelt nur
Blüten zu Früchten.

Du schwebst
mit den fallenden
weißen Blüten,
weit aus der Zeit.

Wenn die Blüten fallen
wirst du schweigen,
und du wirst dich,
still verneigen,
vor der Zeit,
die du nicht greifst.

In the falling snow
of feathery blossom
eternities float
and breathing Time.

Like the soundless whispered
Amen of the dead,
and the silent hope
of love,
the dream of the living.

The silent mouth of life
reveals no secret,
only transforms
blossom into fruit.

You float
with the falling
white blossom,
far out of time.

When the blossom falls
you will be silent,
and you will bow,
in the stillness,
before Time,
which you do not seize.

Elain humain, Figur im Raum
Elain humain, Figure in Space
1975, woodcut, 85 x 60 cm

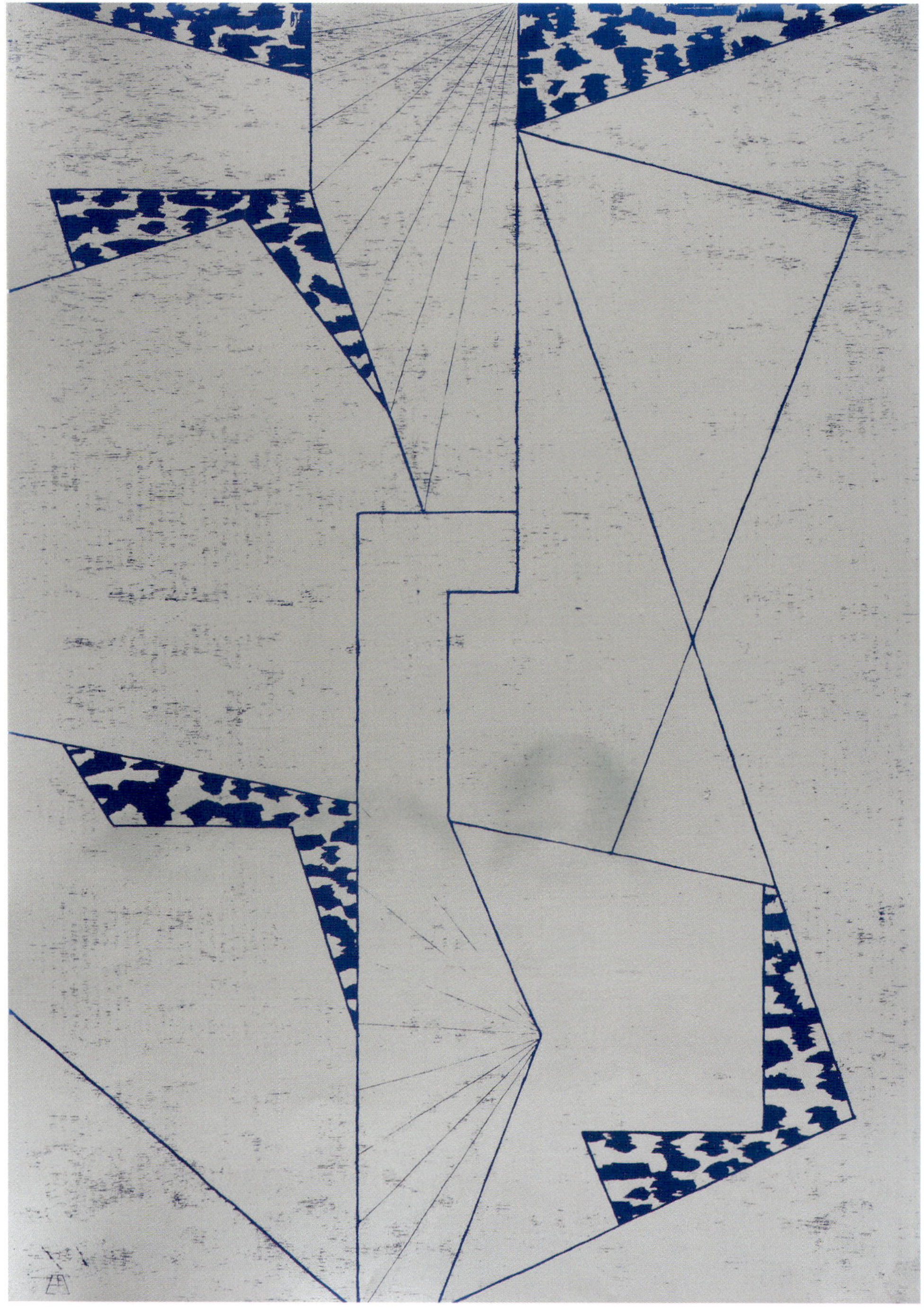

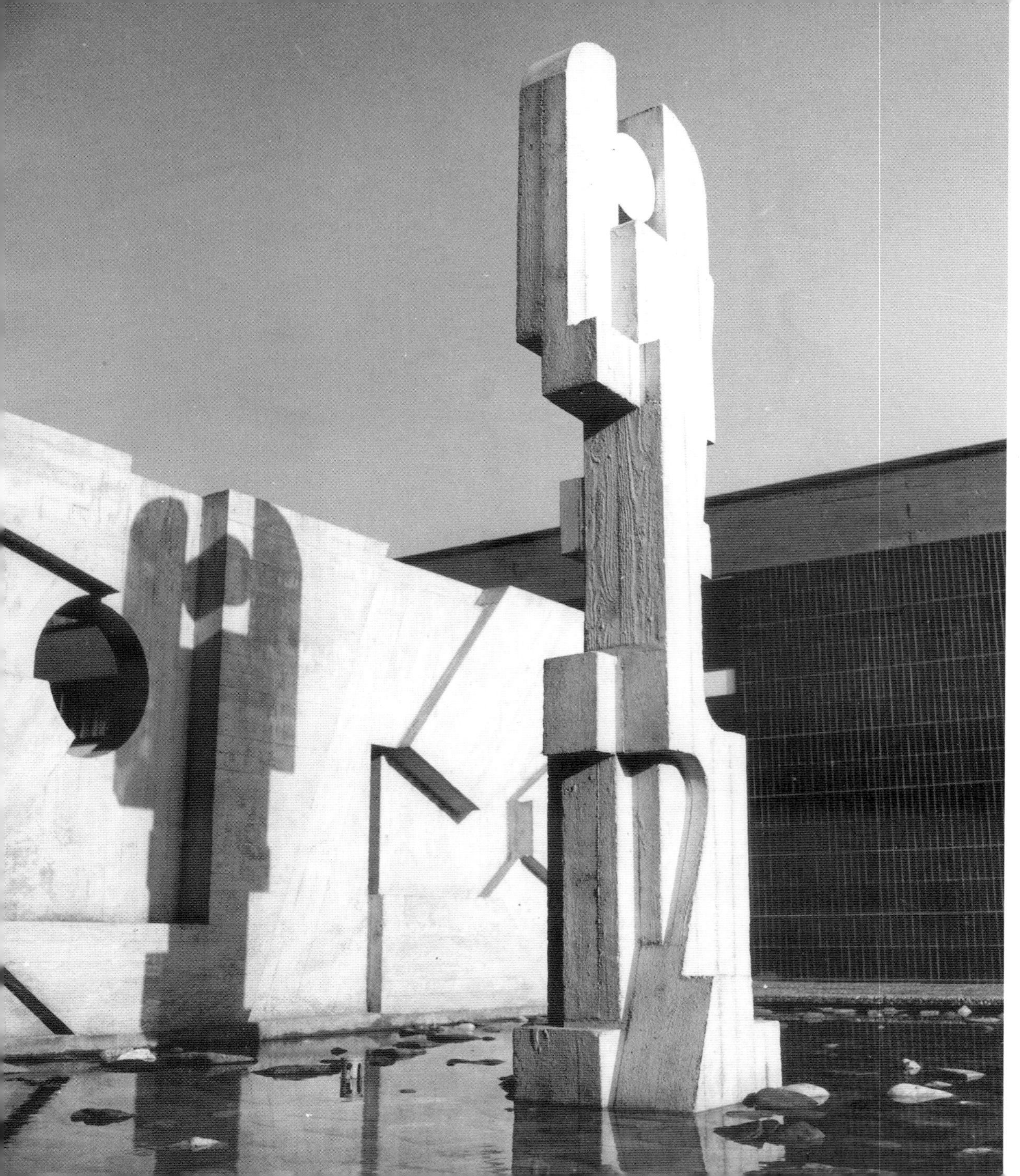

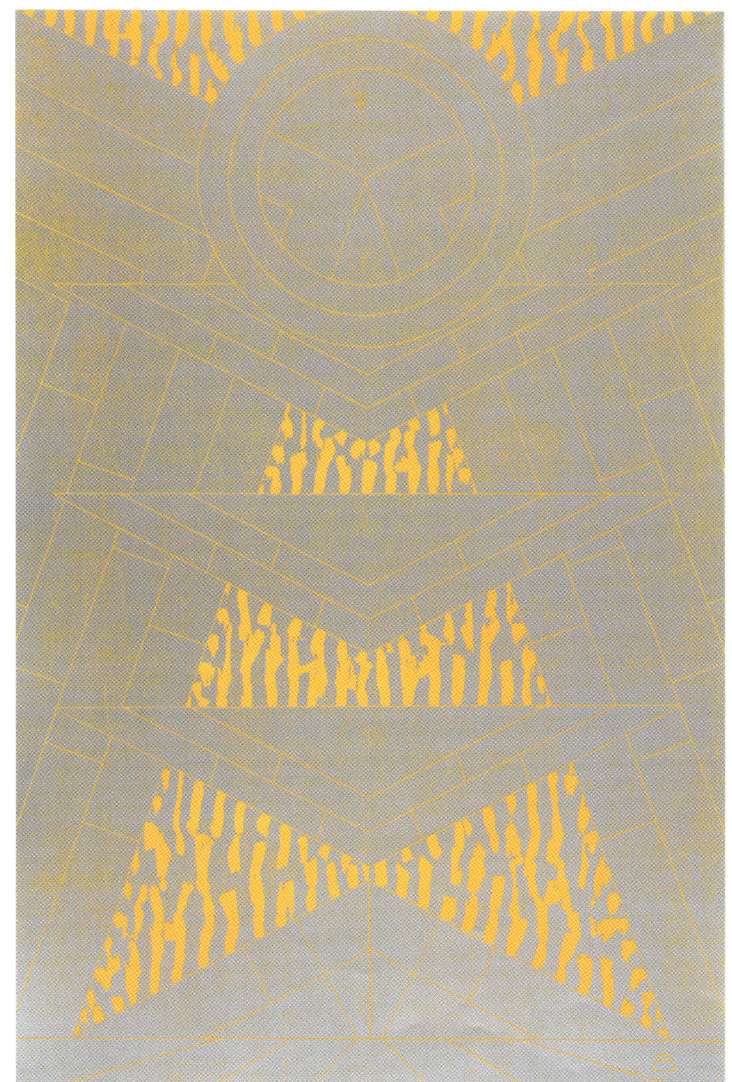

Una Terra Sancta: Flügel der Erde, Manifestation des Lichtes
Una Terra Sancta: Wings of the Earth, Manifestation of Light
1982, woodcut, 90.5 x 60 cm

Opposite: Sonnenwand und Menschenblüte
Sun Wall and Flowering of Humanity
1965, Dyckerhoff concrete, Eltville, Germany (destroyed)

LIGHT

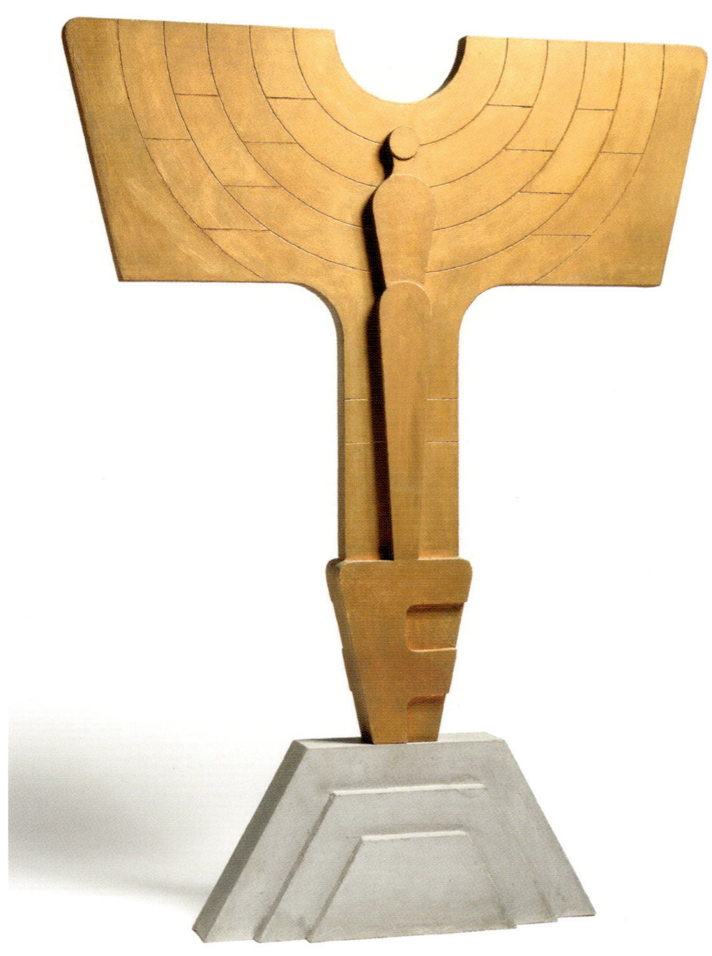

Magna Mater mit Menschenidol
Magna Mater with Human Idol
c. 1971, painted wood, 103 x 78 x 14 cm

MAGNA MATER

Ich bin Europäer
und liebe die Welt,
aus vier Ecken der Erde
floß in mich mein Herzblut.

Ich sah viele Tote,
zerborstene Städte,
blutendes Leid
versperrte den Himmel.

Ich kenne Gewalt,
Schweiß fremder Sonnen
befohlen durch Hunger
den Hahn der Gewehre.

Ich sah die geheimsten Seiten der Menschen,
die Fasern der Not sind mir alle bekannt.

Tief barg ich in mir,
Geheimnis der Mutter,
Herzblut Europas,
die Gewißheit der Liebe.

MAGNA MATER

I am European
and love the world,
from the earth's four corners
the lifeblood flowed into me.

I have seen many dead,
cities torn open,
a blood soaked grief
that blocked the sky.

I know violence,
the sweat of foreign suns
the dictates of hunger
the cocked rifle.

I saw the most secret sides of humanity,
the fibres of despair are all known to me.

I kept deep within me,
the secret of the Mother,
Europa's lifeblood,
the assurance of love.

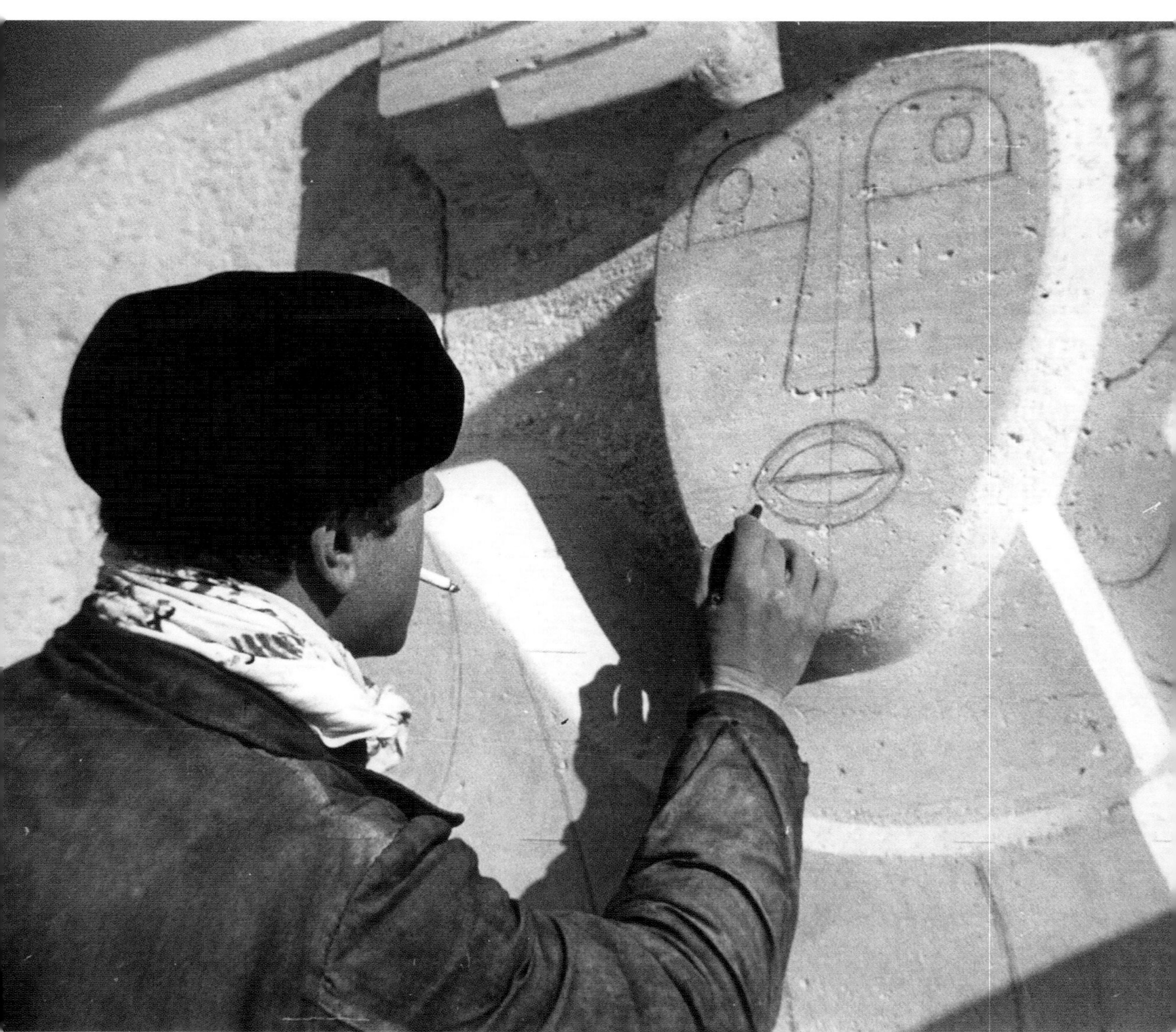

BEGEGNUNG MIT DEM ENGEL

Ich ging den Weg
und folgte meinem Stern,

mit einer Blume
in der Hand.

Nun hab' ich sie verloren.

Ein Engel nahm sie
mit sich fort,
ich gab sie ihm
zum Gruße,
aus meiner sich öffnenden Hand.

In seinem Lächeln
ward mein ganzes Leben
und all mein Traum
geboren neu,

und wurde neues Licht.

ENCOUNTER WITH THE ANGEL

I went my way
and followed my star,

with a flower
in my hand.

Now it is lost.

An angel took it
away with him,
I gave it to him
in greeting,
from my opening hand.

In his smile
my whole life
and all my dream
was born new,

and became new light.

Egon Altdorf at work on *Genius*, for the
Helene Lange Schule, Wiesbaden, c. 1954

„FLÜGEL DER SONNE"
Zur gleichnamigen Skulptur von Egon Altdorf

Aufschwingend und silbern
zieht der Flügel der Sonne,
mit der goldenen Scheibe,
im Schwung seines Bogens.

Sieghaft hoch,
den schwirrenden Traum,
über die Gesetze
der lastenden Erde,

Weltzeichen durchpflügt den Raum.

Nächtliche Strahlung,
aus sich erleuchtend
den Raum,
in nächtlicher Stille.

Herableitend den Regen
und den Segen
über die schlafende Stadt.

'SUN WING'
On the eponymous sculpture by Egon Altdorf

Soaring and silver
the sun's wing,
and the golden disc swept
in the arc of his bow,

high, victorious,
carries the whirring dream
above the laws
of the heavy earth,

world sign ploughs across space.

Nocturnal radiance,
illuminating
space,
in nocturnal stillness.

Channelling down rain
and blessing
on the sleeping city.

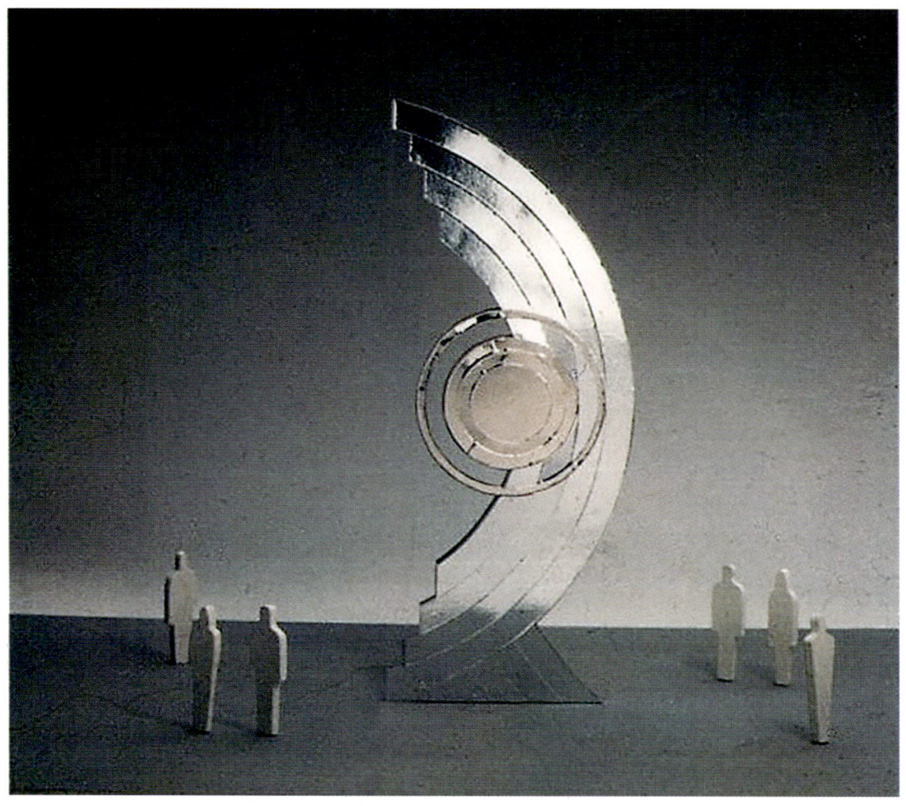

Flügel der Sonne
Sun Wing
1981, cardboard, silver and gold paper, 45 x 17 x 1 cm

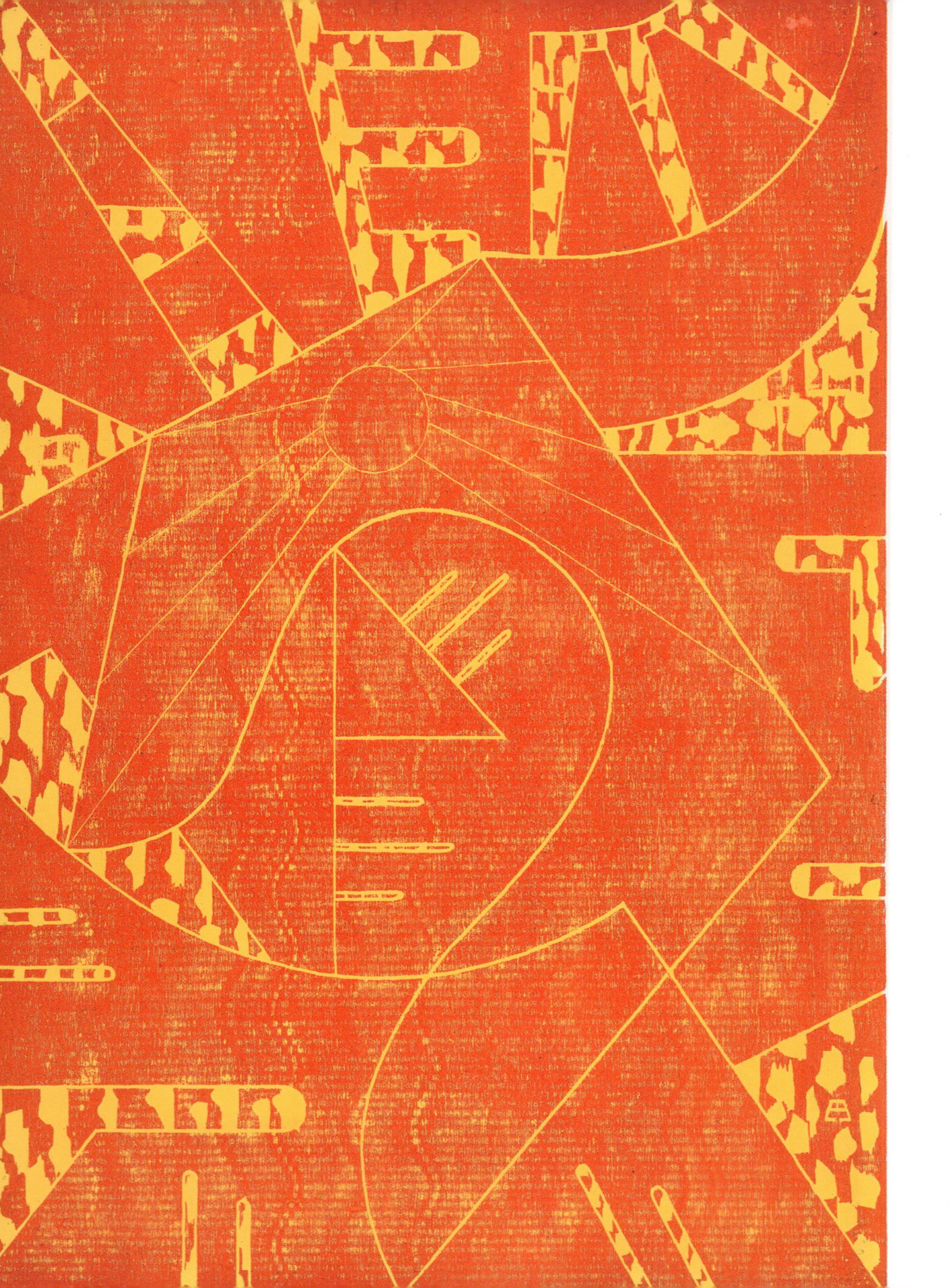

FLÜGEL DER SONNE

Vor dem goldenen Spiegel
deines Lichtes
erblinden Felsen selbst,

sie werden
in deinem Brand
vergehen.

Du warst der Anfang
unseres Seins
und
wirst auch Ende sein.

Dein Flügel
ist die Zeit
und das Gesetz.

Wenn du dich wendest,
war das Leben
Traum.

Ich war ein Teil von dir,
ein Teil des Lichtes,
für kurze Weile.

Aber durch dich
ward ich
ein Mensch
und kannte die Liebe.

SUN WING

Before the golden mirror
of your light
even rocks are blinded,

they will
perish
in your fire.

You were the beginning
of our being
and
will be the end

Your wing
is Time
and Law

When you turn away,
life was
Dream.

I was a part of you,
a part of the light,
for a little while.

But through you
I became
human
and knew love.

Sonnentänzer
Sun Dancer
1968, woodcut, 85 x 60 cm

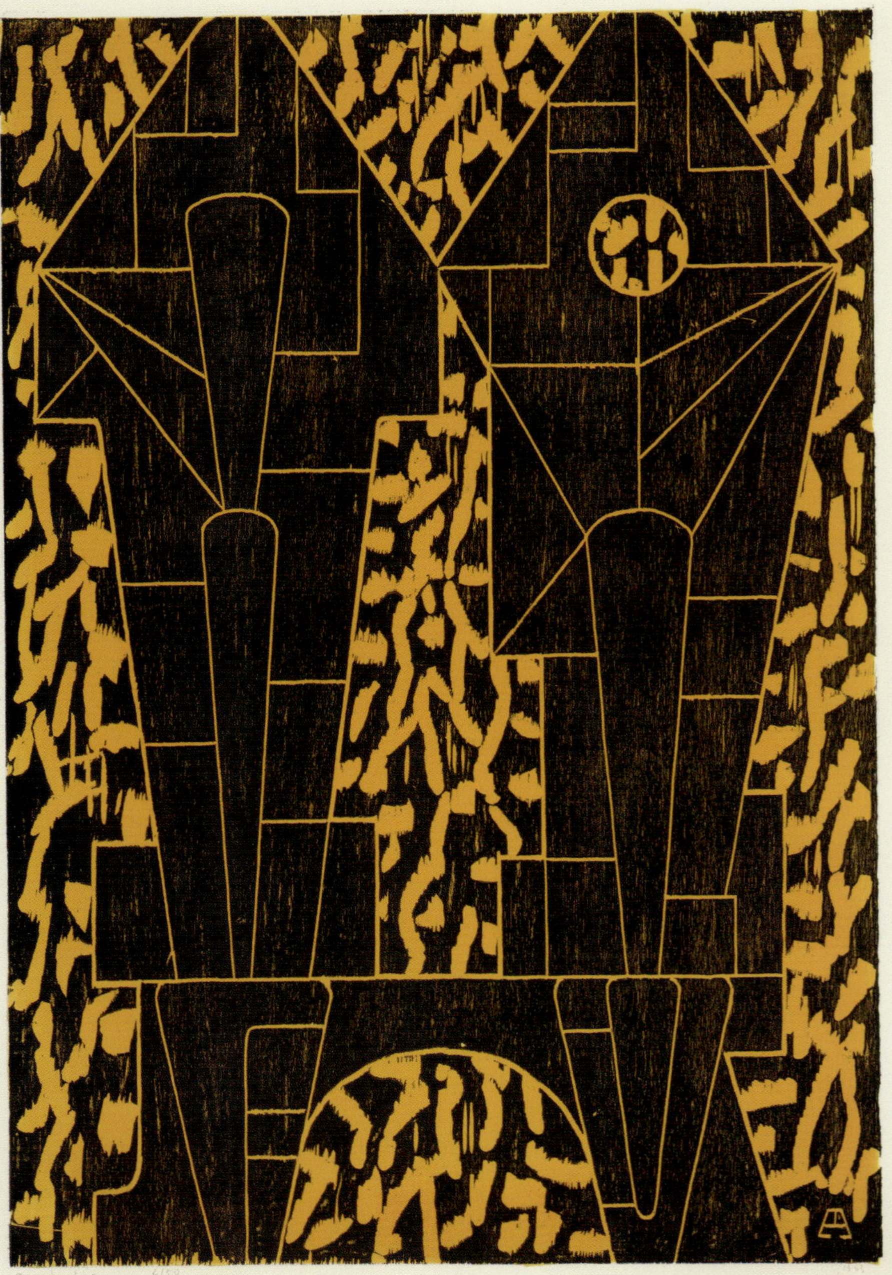

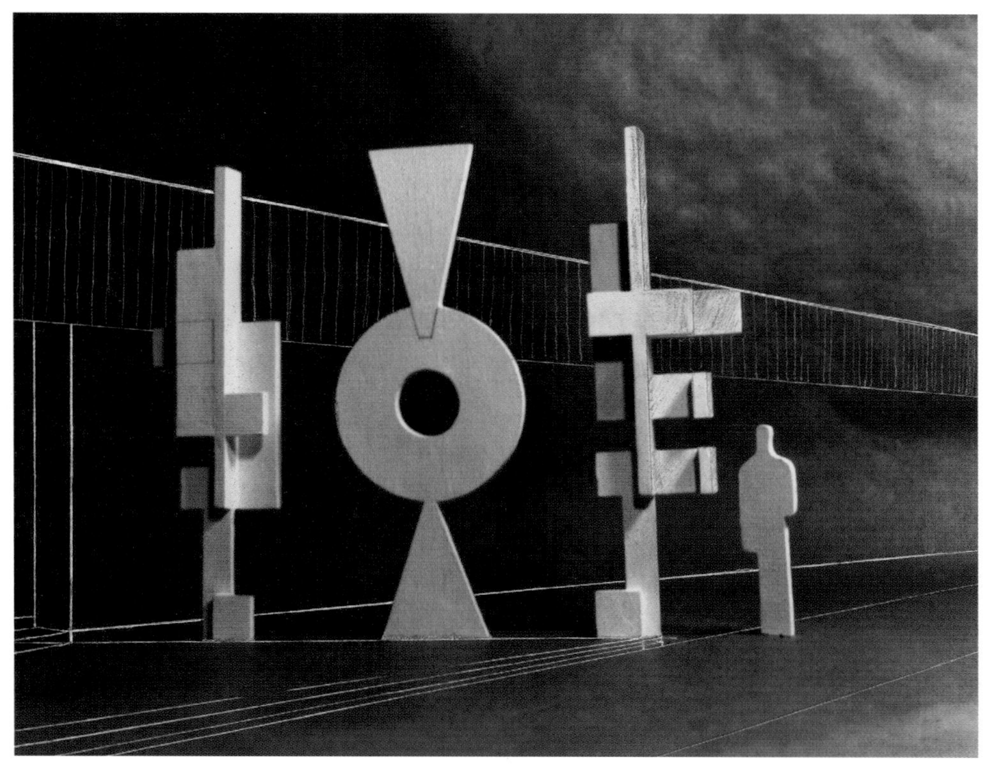

Übermittlung
Transmission
1969, model for concrete,
dimensions and materials unknown

Opposite: Menschentor
Gate of Humanity
1963, woodcut, 84 x 59.5 cm

FOREWORD + AFTERWORD

VORWORT ZU „KREIS DER 7 TORE"

Neben meiner künstlerischen Arbeit
als Bildhauer, Glasgestalter und Holzschneider,
war die Welt der Gedichte mein
ständiger Begleiter, durch jede Zeit.

Mein frühes Studium internationaler,
klassischer und moderner Lyrik entwickelte
in mir ein sehr kritisches
   Bewußtsein von Form und Aussage,
das neue Wege in der deutschen Sprache
finden wollte.

Die häufige Form des Reimes erschien mir bald
als ein Hemnis und zwanghafter, künstlicher
Manierismus.

Ich wollte eine neue, freie,
   melodische, schwingende Sprache,
einfache, liedhafte Schönheit,
eine magische, skaldische Tiefe und die
   transparente,
wechselnde Musikalität von Vokalen und
   Konsonanten.

Die knappe Konstellation der Aussage, Satzbau,
Zeilenbau, Interpunktion, die poetische, starke
Bildhaftigkeit und die Aussagekraft des
   einzelnen
Wortes ergeben die einmalige kostbare Qualität
   eines Gedichtes.

FOREWORD TO 'CIRCLE OF 7 GATES'

Beside my work as an artist, in
sculpture, stained glass and woodcuts,
the world of poetry has been my
constant companion at all times.

My early study of international,
classical and modern poetry developed
in me a very critical awareness of form and
   statement,
that sought new directions
in the German language.

The common form of rhyme soon appeared
to me as a hindrance: an obsessive, artificial
Mannerism.

I wanted a new, free,
   melodic, vibrant language,
a simple, song-like beauty,
a mystical, bardic depth,
   and the transparent,
changeful musicality of vowels
   and consonants.

The pared down constellation of statement, syntax,
line breaks and punctuation, strong,
poetic imagery,
   and the expressive power of the individual word,
yield the unique precious quality
   of a poem.

Manche meiner Gedichte eignen sich zu
klangvoller
Rezitation. Aber viele meiner Gedichte sind
bewußte innerliche Klänge und sollten in ihrer
Sensibilität durch persönliches, meditatives
Lesen aufgenommen werden.

Die Ich-Form in meinen Gedichten ist nicht
egozentrische Position, sondern sie bedeutet
Sprachform „des Menschen", empfunden für alle
und gesprochen aus allen Menschen.

Zum Titel der Ausgabe: Kreis der sieben Tore.
Kreis und Torformen sind wesentliche
Gestaltungs-
elemente meiner künstlerischen Arbeit.

Der „Kreis der sieben Tore" symbolisiert die von
jedem
Menschen zu durchschreitenden
Bewußtseinsstationen
seines Lebens.

Jedes meiner Gedichte sollte neue Sprache zum
Menschen sein, neue Manifestation von Kosmos
und Welt, in ihrem Zauber und ihrer Schönheit,
in brüderlichem Einklang.

Some of my poems lend themselves
to being spoken resonantly
out loud. But in many
of my poems the music is intentionally inward
and their sensibility will emerge
in private, meditative reading.

The 'I' in my poetry is not
egotism, but betokens
'humankind', a way of speaking
that feels for and is spoken by all people.

This book is entitled 'Circle of the Seven Gates'.
Forms based on circles and gateways are
important
structuring elements in my work as an artist.

The 'Circle of the Seven Gates' symbolises
the stages of consciousness
through which every human being
passes in the course
of their life.

Each of my poems should be a new language
for humanity, a new manifestation of cosmos
and world, in their wonder and beauty,
in brotherly harmony.

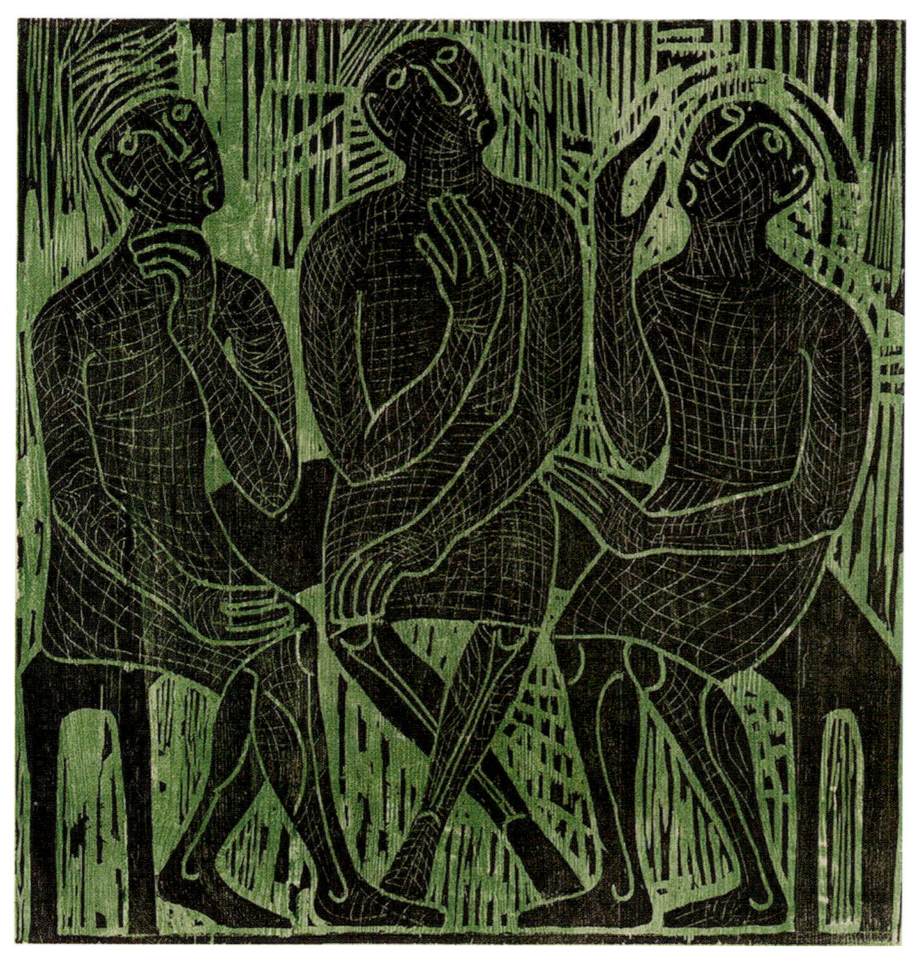

Drei sitzende Männer
Three Seated Men
1952, woodcut, 47 x 45.5 cm

AFTERWORD

This book is meant as an introduction to the work of Egon Altdorf, setting words and images together in a way that lets readers find their own paths and connections within the work or with the world outside it. Sometimes there is an explicit connection between poem and image, but in general the images are not illustrations and the poems are not a commentary.

While it's easy for sculpture and prints, even those based on quite local traditions, to cross language barriers, translating these poems revealed how much they draw on a literary hinterland that is not always well known outside Germany. These notes are intended to give some sense of why that rich landscape might be worth exploring, and of how it relates to all aspects of Altdorf's work, not just the poems.

We have very little information about Altdorf's poetry, other than the poems themselves. There is not much to be gleaned from the few surviving reviews and interviews. We only know that Altdorf was fluent in French and English, is said to have read widely, and that his library was dispersed after his death.

One can read the poems as autobiography: the story of a young man, an only child in a loving family, returning from war and captivity in the knowledge that his parents were dead, their home and everything in it destroyed. His mother died of an untreated illness in the ruins of Berlin. His father had been conscripted, late in the war, when cannon fodder was required to slow the Russian advance, and did not return. The idyllic landscape of Altdorf's childhood, his grandparents' Baltic coastland of Ost Pommern (East Pomerania), was about to be cleansed of its ethnic German population and absorbed into the new Soviet satellite state of Poland. As a prisoner in the US he had been shown film of the death camps. (His reaction was intense anger.) In every sense, the Germany he was returning to had to be built anew.

Or the poems can be read as the story of the long, often difficult unfolding of Altdorf's childhood wish, formed while watching artists painting in picturesque Treptow, to be an artist, 'with a hat'. This also turned out to be a kind of rebuilding, an ongoing search for a new language, as an artist as well as a poet.

The Foreword to the *Circle of 7 Gates* (reprinted here, pp. 102–3), reads as a manifesto, although it was probably written later than many of the poems it precedes, and its instructions aren't always observed. In what way are these poems 'deep' or 'transparent'? What is 'a new language for humanity', or 'a new manifestation of cosmos and world'? Again the questions send us back to the poems.

Whereas Altdorf's sculpture and graphic work clearly engage with that of other living artists, as a poet he seems to have been an outlier. His poems are quite unlike those of his contemporaries: kinder, more utopian, more 'poetic', less astringent, less attentive to the particular, the concrete. They are also prepared to embrace a romantic tradition that was widely seen as hopelessly contaminated by the Nazis (even Hölderlin, suitably redacted, had been issued in a pocket edition for front-line troops). Günter Eich's 1948 poem 'Latrine' rhymes 'Hölderlin' and 'urine'. Altdorf's poems' concerns are usually timeless: artistic creation, love, humanity, the seasons, our relations with God or Nature or the Infinite.

Along with the Bible, four poets – Hölderlin and Novalis writing at the end of the 18th century, Trakl and Rilke reading them at the start of the 20th – seem constantly present in the poems, mirrored in their language and recurring themes. (I don't suggest that Altdorf's reading was confined to these writers, only that their influence appears particularly strong, and worth examining.) One aspect they share, which was clearly part of their attraction to Altdorf, is a kind of tenderness. Their intellectual foundation was laid by the philosopher Immanuel Kant (1724–1804), whose work also seems central to Altdorf's poems.[1]

Kant, a scientist self-confessedly 'in love with metaphysics', saw the endless blood-soaked religious controversies over matters that, by their nature, cannot

1 These notes are particularly indebted to four books, listed below in Further Reading, by T. J. Reed (on Kant and the Enlightenment), Wm. Arctander O'Brien (on Novalis), Richard Sieburth (on Hölderlin), and Alexander Stillmark (on Trakl). All translations in this essay are the author's own.

be known as a fatal diversion from the real task of building a community based on respect for human dignity, independent thought and debate: the project of the *Aufklärung*, or Enlightenment. Kant's achievement, fundamental because it undermined the God-given authority of church and state, was to mark out the limits of what can and cannot be known: the inherent limitations of the human mind, the way human perception is structured by time and space, and the conditions for processing the raw materials conveyed by the senses.

Kantian and Enlightenment concepts crop up like bedrock in Altdorf's poems: a God derived from ethics (rather than vice versa); the brotherhood of Man; a European civilisation free of warfare; the then new concept of human dignity, around which was constructed the 1949 Basic Law, still the foundation of the German state, and intended to make impossible any return to National Socialism. Odd words in the poems, sometimes used in an unexpected way, suggest Kant and the 18th century: *brüderlich* (brotherly), *Gesetz* (law), *Gestirn* (heavenly body), *Mensch* (human being), *Schema* (pattern).[2]

Kant's very personal conclusion to his *Critique of Practical Reason* (*Kritik der praktischen Vernunft*, 1788) could be used to sum up Altdorf's poems:

Two things fill the mind with ever new and increasing admiration and awe, the more often and steadily one thinks about them: the starry sky above me and the moral law within me. I see them both before me and connect them directly with the consciousness of my existence.

This is simultaneously an acceptance of mortality (Kant was a cosmologist, at ease with the vastness and impersonality of the universe) and an assertion of an independent moral self. Altdorf's inscription, written and

---

2 There are Rilkean words too: *Wandlung* (transformation), *Figur* (figure); Rilkean compounds: *Herzatem* (heart breath), *Knabenhand* (boy's hand), the moon-tree, the sun plough; and metaphors: *die Stille wie eine Wand*, the stillness like a wall; the angel materialising as *ein furchtbarer Fels*, a fearsome cliff face. There are words and images from Novalis of signs, messengers, mediators, networks; *Geflecht* (woven mesh), *Bote* (messenger), *Botschaft* (tidings), *Korrespondenz*, *Vielzahl* (manifold), *Spiegel* (mirror), and from Trakl: *Asphalt*, *Traum* (dream), *silbern* (silver), *Abend* (evening), *kristallen* (crystal), schweigsam (sleepy), *milde* (mild), *Stille* (stillness), *Flügel* (wing), *Verwesung* (decay), *Herbst* (autumn), *Umnachtung* (derangement).

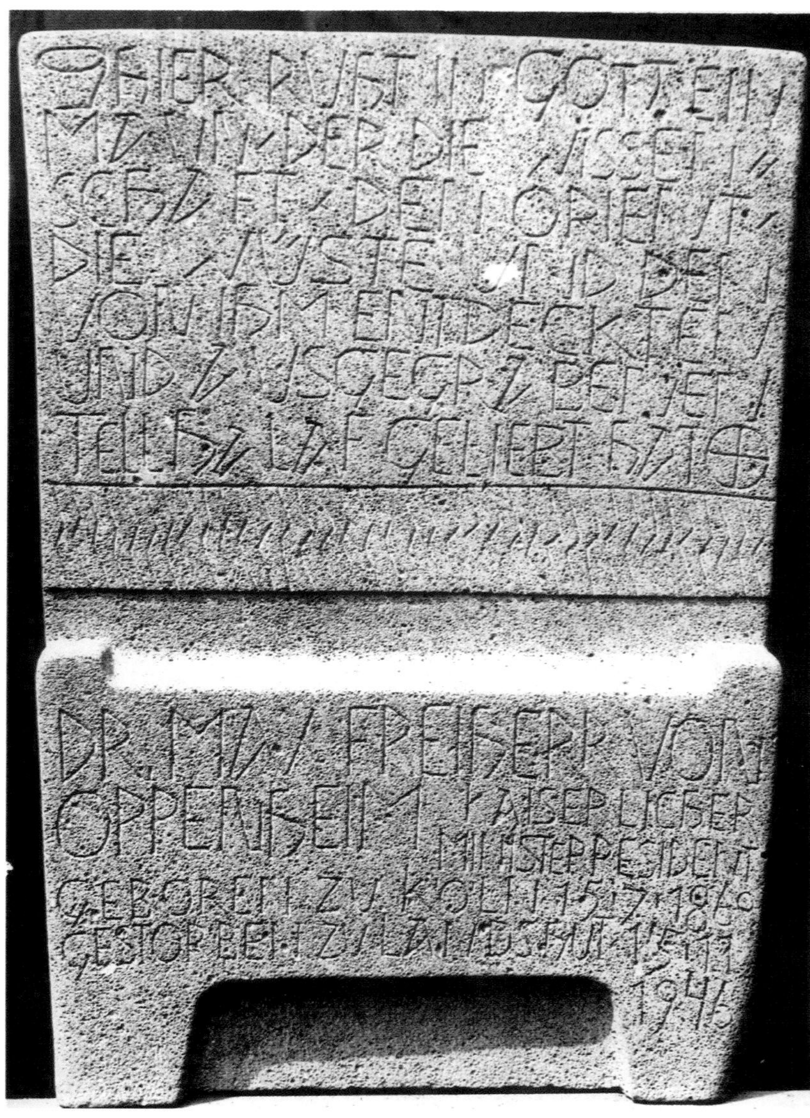

Memorial to Max Freiherr von
Oppenheim, basalt, 1951

carved by him in 1953 on a stela marking the site of the destroyed synagogue at Wiesbaden, reads: DER WELTGEWISSEN IST DIE LIEBE, the conscience of the world is love.

Hölderlin (b. 1770) and Novalis (b. 1772) were almost exact contemporaries. Both rejected the secular humanism and neo-classicism of Goethe and Schiller, as well as the Protestant pietism of their upbringing, for a syncretic vision that apparently reconciled pantheism with Christianity. Both lived their lives with an intensity that is inseparable from their work. Novalis died at the age of 28 in 1801. Hölderlin lived until 1843, but in 1807 suffered a mental collapse that incapacitated him as a poet.

Altdorf could fairly be called a disciple of Novalis. His poems are steeped in Novalis's language and philosophy, and in a poem dedicated to him in *Way and Star* (*Weg und Stern*, 2001), Altdorf wrote: 'You carried my life along with you,/ and my brotherly love/ carried you, like a precious star.'

Friedrich von Hardenberg (1772–1801), known as Novalis (a pen name he barely used), was a poet, novelist, lawyer, administrator, mining engineer and a passionate student of mathematics, physics, chemistry and philosophy. His politics were revolutionary, his Romantic religion described by the theologian Karl Barth as 'dangerous' and 'menacing'. In his short life of not quite 29 years he published very little, and his brilliant and extensive writings, often unfinished or deliberately written in fragmentary form, were manipulated after his death to present a more acceptable and marketable product. His liking for irony made this easier.

Novalis is still mythologised as the ultimate Romantic poet, the lover of the Blue Flower, yearning after the unattainable, morbidly in love with his own mortality and the prospect of mystic reunion with his dead fiancée, an image that obscures his extraordinary modernity, breadth of achievement, subversive energy and intellectual acuity. Novalis's more modern reputation is as a pioneering philosopher of language, whose poetic prose, as much as his verse, has inspired painters, poets and musicians from Richard Wagner to Max Ernst, Paul Klee, Jorge Luis Borges and the French Surrealists.

Novalis's interest in language began as an inquiry into the semiotics of Kant and Johann Gottlieb Fichte, in the course of which he came to see language's participation in illusion as a source of power. Words, he became convinced, don't merely interpret the world, but themselves change it. This is the philosophical basis for the high value he, and eventually the whole Romantic movement, placed on fiction. It now seems clear (though in Altdorf's time it probably was not) that even before most of his poetry and fiction was written, Novalis already held the view that 'God', 'morality' and 'love' are inherently human constructions, exposed to the workings of power.

Novalis's fascination with language and representation is linked to the myth of Orpheus, which suggests that poetry, with language and music, is a form of power. Orpheus, with his song, tames beasts and moves rocks and trees. He gains entry to the underworld to rescue Eurydice, his wife, but loses her by looking back at her. Torn in pieces by the Maenads, his head floats down the river still singing, then comes to rest in a cave, uttering prophecies until Apollo finally silences it. The lyre is taken up to heaven to become one of the constellations.

The myth of Orpheus is ambiguous, self-questioning and endlessly productive. It concerns the relationship of man to nature, implying a poetic power – to subjugate nature, to prophesy, even to triumph over death. Orpheus is poet, philosopher, taxonomist, scientist. He is the subject of two poems by Altdorf, and of Rilke's sequence, *The Sonnets to Orpheus* (*Die Sonette an Orpheus*, 1923), and of the poem *Orpheus, Eurydice, Hermes* in the *New Poems* (*Neue Gedichte*, 1907). Orpheus is also present in this opening passage of *The Novices of Saïs* (*Die Lehrlinge zu Saïs*), two fragments of a nominally unfinished novel written around 1778, which has relevance to Altdorf's sculpture and woodcuts as well as to his poems. Its themes are language and its capacity to deceive; nature as language, with its own elusive grammar (as figures, as a cypher); poetry as a form of magical power.

Men walk various paths. He who follows and compares them will see miraculous figures arise, figures that seem to belong to that great cypher which we see everywhere, on wings, on eggshells, on clouds, in snow, in crystals and in stone formations, upon freezing water; on the inside and outside of mountains, of plants, of beasts, of men; in the lights of the heavens, in markings on the smooth surfaces (Scheiben) of pitch and glass, in patterns of iron filings round a magnet, and in strange conjunctions of chance. In them we sense a key to this miraculous script, even to its grammar, but the sense will not take on any clear form and seems unwilling to become a higher key. […]

[Our teacher] told us often how as a child the urge to make the fullest use of all his senses left him no peace. He looked at the stars and traced in the sand their courses, their conjunctions. Unremittingly he looked into the sea or air above him, and never tired of watching its clarity, its movements, its clouds, its lights. He gathered stones, flowers, beetles of all kinds, and laid them in rows, in many different ways. To men and animals he paid close attention, he sat on the shores of the sea, looking for shells. To his feelings and his thoughts he listened closely. He knew not whither his yearnings drew him. When he grew older he was free to roam, to see other lands and other seas, new skies, new stars, unknown plants, animals and people, to descend into caves, to see how the earth was built in shelves and multicoloured layers, and clay pressed into curious rock formations. Everywhere he found what was familiar, but weirdly mingled or combined, and in this way strange things would often order themselves in him. Now he began to notice connections everywhere, meeting points, coincidences. Soon he saw nothing in isolation. The perceptions of his senses crowded into large vividly coloured images: he heard, saw, touched and thought, all at once. He loved to bring strangers together. Sometimes he saw stars as people, or people as stars, stones as animals, clouds as plants, he played with powers and appearances, he knew where and how to find this or that, and could make it appear, and with his own hands sought out tones and passages in the strings.

We know, from the recollections of Altdorf's friends, that Hölderlin's poems were important to him. Given their quality, that's unsurprising. But Altdorf's poems don't resemble Hölderlin's in any obvious way, not least because no one else, unless perhaps occasionally Rilke or Trakl, ever actually *sounds* like Hölderlin. There may be miniature exceptions: Christopher Middleton has noted Hölderlin's sensitivity 'to the oscillations of light (frequently expressed by the acute shimmer of the verb *glänzen*)' and 'to barely perceptible rustlings and rushings (*säuseln, rauschen*)',[3] words that bring to mind Altdorf's poem

3 Christopher Middleton, quoted in Sieburth, 'Introduction' to Friedrich Hölderlin, *Hymns and Fragments*, p. 42.

Evening (*Abend*). There are other poems by Altdorf, such as *My Origin* (*Mein Herkommen*), whose structure might derive from Hölderlin.

But in general, Hölderlin's influence is tonal and thematic. 'Hölderlin's entire oeuvre', says Richard Sieburth, 'pursues a precarious dialogue with the Other.' In Paris, visiting a collection of Greek statuary, Hölderlin discovered

the same fusion of clarity and conflagration, of vulnerability and vigor, that he had observed in the landscape and inhabitants of southern France. He was struck above all by the "tenderness" (Zärtlichkeit) of the Greek body, by the delicacy of its stamina; and in the silent, ingathered poise of classical sculpture – intense movement coinciding with repose, fire informing each definition of detail – he discerned the essential feature of all great art. Such certainty of purpose, such self-assurance, he noted, was the supreme kind of representation, "the highest form of the sign." [4]

David Constantine describes Hölderlin as

the poet of absence. His gods have departed, presence has been lost. There is no poet more honest and uncompromising in the depiction of absence and loss. Reading Hölderlin we know what bereavement, in its widest sense, is like. But we know also, with an equal or greater force, what fulfilment would be like, what it would be like to live lives full of love and joy; and the injunction of his poetry, always there, is to believe in the possibility of that fulfilment and to seek to make it real. [5]

These themes of Otherness, of absence, and of tenderness – in a human body, in sculpture, in a landscape – are shared by Altdorf, as is, sometimes, the sense of loss, and Hölderlin's Hellenism, his linking of Christianity to older or archaic civilisations.

Georg Trakl (1887–1914) and Rainer Maria Rilke (1875–1926) are poets of the early 20th century, each with a mature style that is unique and unmistakeable. The rediscovered late poems of Hölderlin became available around 1912, when Rilke was beginning his *Duino Elegies* (*Duineser Elegien*, 1923), and both poets fell under their spell. In 1914 Rilke wrote a poem addressing Hölderlin with great affection.

---

4 Sieburth, ibid., p. 12.
5 David Constantine, 'Introduction' to Friedrich Hölderlin, *Selected Poems*, p. 10.

What did Altdorf take from them?

In Rilke's case, since Altdorf's poem dedicated to him is very early (*see* p. 25), the answer might well be his sense of vocation as an artist and poet. The poem refers to hands, therefore to things made as well as written. Altdorf would have been attracted by Rilke's own fascination with the visual, with Rodin and the processes of casting bronze, and by Rilke's own agile new language of space and interiority, with its ability to move between human experience, the external world, and the world of myth, using one to express the other. Inevitably, Altdorf is never so at home in that language as Rilke himself, but the angels in Altdorf's poems have much in common with Rilke's, and there is a strangely relaxed Rilkean tenderness in some of the poems that is also evident in some of Altdorf's earlier carvings and woodcuts, such as the *Three Seated Men* (p. 104).

This interchange of the verbal and material can be traced back to Kant and Novalis, but reaches a new level in Rilke, as if a pattern of thought can be realised at will in words or in, say, sculpture. The sculptor Richard Deacon, reading Rilke's *Sonnets to Orpheus* in 1978, began to make drawings that were related to the poems but not literal representations of any aspect of them. Their collective title was *It's Orpheus when there's singing*. Later he made sculptures, also related. Deacon uses the words 'resonance' and 'equivalence', which suggest a process of translation.

Rilke's Orphism is closely connected with that of Novalis. It is, among other things, a kind of secular magic. Thom Gunn wrote, in 1973, from his own experience, on the process of writing a poem:

I think – in all seriousness and not as a mere playful metaphor, it is also connected with the processes of magic. It is a reaching out into the unexplained areas of the mind, in which the air is too thickly primitive or too fine for us to live continually. From that reaching I bring back loot, and don't always know at first what that loot is, except that I hope that it is of value as an understanding or as a talisman, or more likely as a combination of the two, of both rational power and irrational.[6]

---

6 Gunn, 'Writing a Poem' (1973), in *Strong Words: Modern Poets on Modern Poetry*, ed. W. N. Herbert & Matthew Hollis, Bloodaxe Books, 2000, p. 142.

Hölderlin's Christianity was shared by Trakl, but not by Rilke. Trakl was probably much nearer to orthodoxy than Hölderlin, though his sense of alienation and loss was no less acute.

Of the four poets in question here, Trakl is the only one to have experienced actual warfare, as Altdorf did. Unusually among European poets in 1914 (Rilke included), he had no illusions about its nature. Qualified as a pharmacist, he joined up in 1914 as an orderly in the Medical Corps. After the battle of Grodek in Galicia he was placed in sole charge of 90 gravely wounded soldiers in a makeshift field hospital without medical support. The experience led directly to his death, by taking an overdose of cocaine while suffering from depression.

Trakl's vision was much darker than that of Novalis or Rilke. His poems do not exclude hope, but contain death and corruption, dissolution and decay, transience and pain. His imagery is concrete and exact, concerned, like Altdorf's, with what lies beyond the visible, but more deeply rooted in the sensuous self and the palpable world. There is a fruitful tension between harmony and disharmony, the metallic and the mellifluous.

After Trakl's death in 1915, Rilke admiringly described him as an 'excluded being' who 'experienced even what was close at hand as though pressed against panes of glass'. Trakl's purity, precision and striving for absolute truth of expression would fulfil (and perhaps even suggested) Altdorf's aims in his 'Foreword' (pp. 102–3). Altdorf's rhythms are quite different, his achievement not truly comparable, but the best of his poems often seem closer to Trakl than to any other model.

What conclusions can we draw?

First, that Altdorf's poems tell us something about his work as an artist. German Romanticism was fascinated by transformations, evolution, mirroring, connections, relation, translation (between languages and between media), and by language, signs, messages, cyphers, inscriptions. Altdorf's titles are evidence. Christian iconography was part of this, as were the musical patterns played by stringed instruments, or described in the

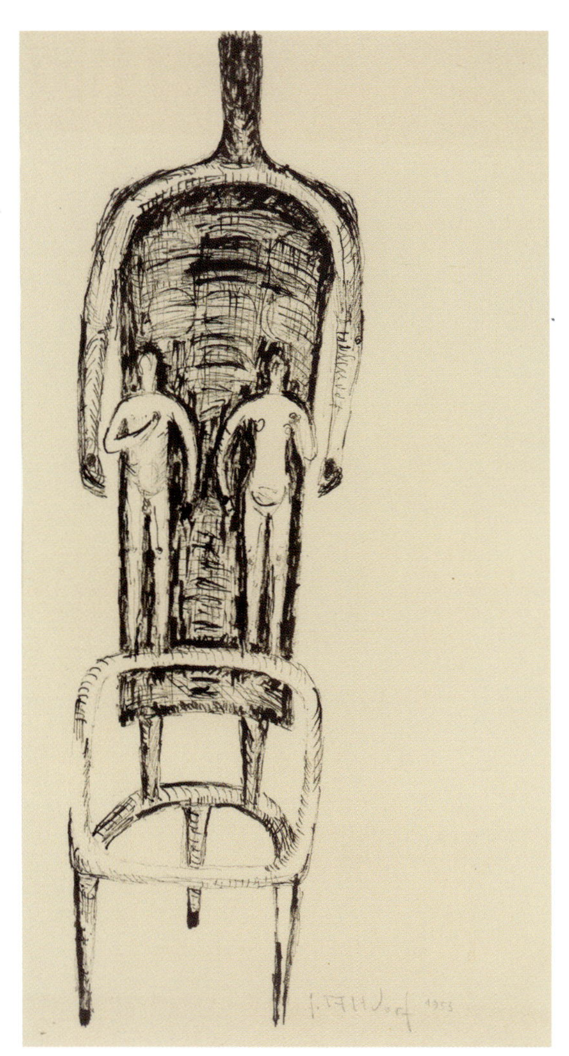

Schöpfung
Creation
1953, ink on paper, 68.5 x 20.5 cm

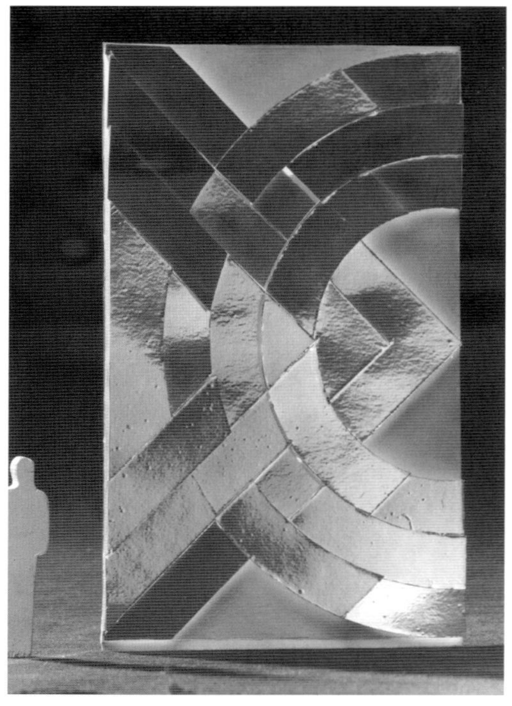 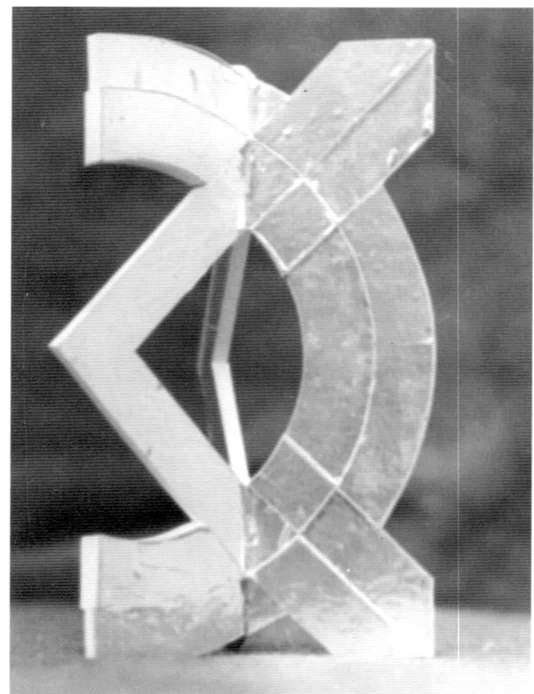

Lichtwand
Light Wall
1973, maquettes in cardboard and
silver paper for unrealised rotating
steel sculpture (destroyed)

Novices of Saïs, or formed in our own minds. (Poems and translated poems are also patterns.) I'd suggest that source material for the poems was, at least equally, source material for drawings, prints or sculptures.

Second, that Altdorf's decision in the 1940s or 50s to ally himself with the generation of the 1770s, the earliest modernists, was unusual and likely to have been carefully considered. He must have seen this as a new beginning that was also compatible with the strong Christian faith he shared, at least in part, with Trakl and Hölderlin, if not Novalis. It seems possible that Altdorf's early interest in Rilke (whose own convictions were more Nietzschean than Christian) led him to those earlier poets, including Trakl, whom Rilke himself admired. Did Altdorf's own beliefs (which may have changed with time) reflect those of Novalis, who was capable of such aphorisms as 'The artist is thoroughly irreligious – he can therefore work in religion as in bronze'?[1] This is not to question the genuineness of Altdorf's commitment, only to be curious about its nature. Trakl's Christianity was something else again, and today's Novalis, after many years of academic revaluation, will certainly differ from the Novalis available to Altdorf in 1950.

The choices being made by writers in the post-war years were not straightforward. Romanticism, of any kind, could be held responsible for Nazism, as could the whole project of the Enlightenment. Hölderlin began to be rehabilitated, as a left-leaning figure, only in the 1960s. Whatever his degree of scepticism, there is commitment and integrity in Altdorf's alignment of his own beliefs as an artist and poet with the Kantian morality of the Basic Law and the Christianity in which he was brought up.

Altdorf's dedication to the *Circle of 7 Gates* is an epitaph to his parents:

Die Sonne verglüht im See,
ein Vogel irrt durch den Abend
sein Rufen verstummt an den Ufern.

The sun's glow sinks in the lake,
a stray bird flies through the evening,
its cry falls silent on the shores.

Michael Trevor

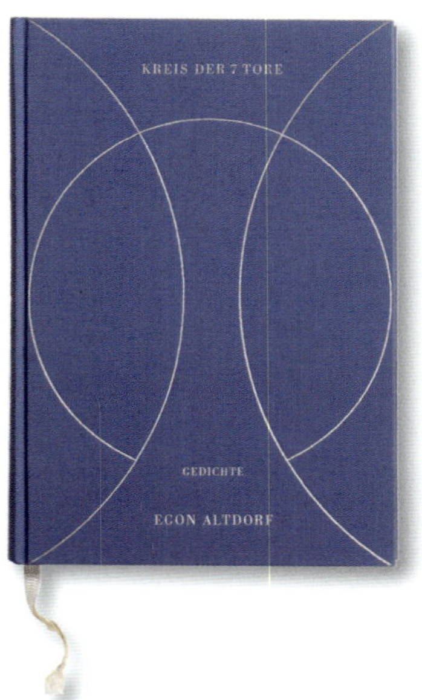

FURTHER READING

ALTDORF

Egon Altdorf
— *Kreis der 7 Tore*, Köllmann, Wiesbaden, 1995
— *Traum von Leben*, Köllmann, Wiesbaden, 2000
— *Weg und Stern*, Köllmann, Wiesbaden, 2001

www.egonaltdorf.org

Into the Light: The Art of Egon Altdorf, ed. Judith LeGrove, Sansom & Company, 2023
Egon Altdorf 1922–2008: Die Kunst der inneren Erneuerung: Skulptur, Grafik, Glasfenster, Lyrik,
        ed. Judith LeGrove and Felicitas Reusch, Reichert Verlag, 2022

KANT

T. J. Reed, *Light in Germany: Scenes from an Unknown Enlightenment*, University of Chicago Press, 2015

NOVALIS

Novalis, *Hymns to the Night*, trans. Dick Higgins, Treacle Press, 1978
Novalis, *The Novices of Saïs*, trans. Ralph Manheim, drawings by Paul Klee, 1949,
        new ed. Archipelago, 2010
W. A. O'Brien, *Novalis: Signs of Revolution*, Duke University Press, 1995
Penelope Fitzgerald, *The Blue Flower*, Flamingo, 1995

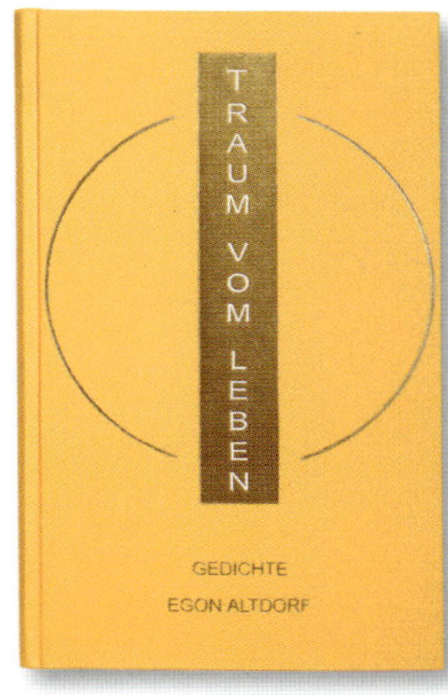 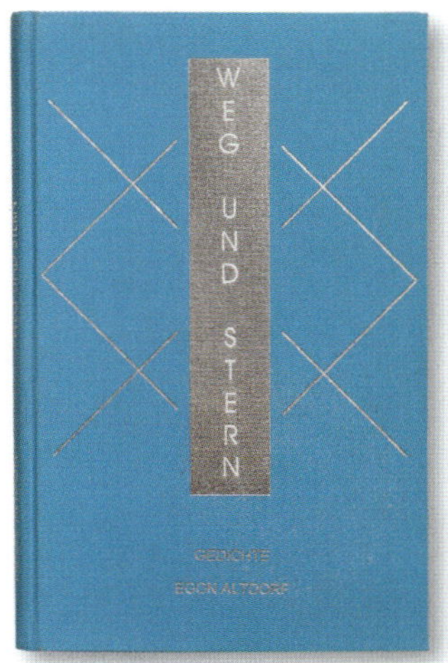

Cover designs for the three published poetry volumes

RILKE

Don Paterson, *Orpheus: a version of Rilke's Die Sonette an Orpheus*, Faber, 2006
Rainer Maria Rilke, *New Poems*, trans. Edward Snow, North Point Press, 2001
An Unofficial Rilke: Poems 1912–1926, trans. Michael Hamburger, Anvil Press Poetry, 1981
W. H. Gass, *Reading Rilke: Reflections on the Problems of Translation*, A. A. Knopf, 1999
Jo Shapcott, *Tender Taxes: Versions of Rilke's French Poems*, Faber, 2001

TRAKL

Georg Trakl, *Poems and Prose*, trans. Alexander Stillmark, Libris, 2001

HÖLDERLIN

Friedrich Hölderlin, *Selected Poems*, trans. David Constantine, Bloodaxe Books, 1990
Friedrich Hölderlin, *Hymns and Fragments*, trans. Richard Sieburth, Princeton University Press, 1984

ANTHOLOGIES

The Poetry of Survival: Post-War Poets of Central and Eastern Europe, ed. Daniel Weissbort, Anvil Press Poetry, 1991
The Faber Book of 20th-Century German Poems, ed. Michael Hofmann, Faber, 2005

GENERAL

Michael Hamburger, *Reason and Energy: Studies in German Literature*, Weidenfeld & Nicolson, rev. ed., 1970

Sources

The poems on pages 13, 15, 23, 25, 31 and 60 are previously unpublished.
Zu Rembrandts Gemälde (p. 29) was published in *Egon Altdorf 1922–2008: Die Kunst der inneren Erneuerung* (2022) and in English in *Into the Light: The Art of Egon Altdorf* (2023). *Traum* (p. 41) was published in *Weg und Stern* (2000). The remaining poems were published in *Kreis der 7 Tore* (1995). Unless stated otherwise, all art works are by Egon Altdorf, in the collection of the artist's estate.

Acknowledgements

Thanks are due to Dorian Crone, Nicolette David, Gerd Schulz, and the book's designer, Simon Bishop, and publisher, Clara Hudson. Egon Altdorf always looked to the future. This book is dedicated to his grandchildren: Lucy, Alexander and Gabriel.

Credits

Artist's archive, photographer unknown: pp. 2, 5, 12, 22, 26, 41, 44, 59, 75, 79, 90, 97, 116; W. Hegge: pp. 57 (right), 82; Hilde Laskawy: cover photograph, pp. 30, 57 (left, centre), 94, 101; Heinrich Pieroth: p. 108; Staatliche Museen zu Berlin, Gemäldegalerie / Christoph Schmidt (cc): p. 28; Staatliche Museen zu Berlin, Nationalgalerie / Andres Kilger (cc): p. 14. All other photographs are by Douglas Atfield.